Human Rights

Opposing Viewpoints®

OTHER BOOKS OF RELATED INTEREST

OPPOSING VIEWPOINTS SERIES

America's Victims
Censorship
Central America
Child Welfare
Civil Liberties
The Death Penalty
Discrimination
Feminism
The Homeless
Homosexuality
Illegal Immigration
Immigration
Israel
The Middle East
Population
Race Relations
Social Justice
The Third World

CURRENT CONTROVERSIES SERIES

Ethics
Free Speech
Gay Rights
Illegal Immigration
Minorities
Nationalism and Ethnic Conflict
Native American Rights
Police Brutality
Racism

AT ISSUE SERIES

Ethnic Conflict
Gay Marriage
Immigration Policy
The United Nations
U.S. Policy Toward China

Human Rights
Opposing Viewpoints ®

David L. Bender, *Publisher*
Bruno Leone, *Executive Editor*
Brenda Stalcup, *Managing Editor*
Scott Barbour, *Senior Editor*
Mary E. Williams, *Book Editor*

OPPOSING
VIEWPOINTS®
SERIES

Greenhaven Press, Inc., San Diego, California

Cover photo: Sue Streeter, Tony Stone

Library of Congress Cataloging-in-Publication Data

Human rights : opposing viewpoints / Mary E. Williams, book editor.
    p.   cm. — (Opposing viewpoints series)
  Includes bibliographical references and index.
  ISBN 1-56510-797-7 (lib. : alk. paper). —
ISBN 1-56510-796-9 (pbk. : alk. paper)
  1. Human rights. I. Williams, Mary E., 1960–   .
II. Series: Opposing viewpoints series (Unnumbered)
JC571.H76968 1998
323—dc21   97-51706
                                                            CIP

Greenhaven Press, Inc., P.O. Box 289009
San Diego, CA 92198-9009

"CONGRESS SHALL MAKE NO LAW. . . ABRIDGING THE FREEDOM OF SPEECH, OR OF THE PRESS."

First Amendment to the U.S. Constitution

The basic foundation of our democracy is the First Amendment guarantee of freedom of expression. The Opposing Viewpoints Series is dedicated to the concept of this basic freedom and the idea that it is more important to practice it than to enshrine it.

Contents

Why Consider Opposing Viewpoints?   9

Introduction   12

Chapter 1: How Should Human Rights Be Defined?

Chapter Preface   16

1. Human Rights Are Universal   17
   Pierre Sané

2. A Universal Definition of Human Rights Ignores Cultural Diversity   21
   Bilahari Kausikan

3. International Human Rights Standards Neglect Asian Values   25
   Robert Weil

4. International Human Rights Standards Are Relevant to Asian Societies   33
   Xiaorong Li

5. A Human Rights Agenda Must Include Women's Rights   44
   Hillary Rodham Clinton

6. The Women's Rights Agenda Ignores Third World Concerns   51
   Anne Applebaum

Periodical Bibliography   57

Chapter 2: What Is the State of Human Rights?

Chapter Preface   59

1. The United States Faces Human Rights Challenges   60
   John Shattuck

2. The United States Deserves No Criticism on Human Rights   67
   Midge Decter

3. The Use of Child Labor Violates Human Rights   74
   Bruce Weiner

4. The Use of Child Labor Does Not Always Violate Human Rights   81
   Shahidul Alam

5. Refugees Face Barriers to Political Asylum   88
   Amnesty International

6. Many Claims of Refugee Status Are Unwarranted   98
David Simcox

7. The Use of Land Mines Violates Human Rights   108
Karen J. Longstreth

8. Outlawing Land Mines Would Be Futile   112
Bernard E. Trainor

Periodical Bibliography   115

Chapter 3: What Should Be Done to Stop Human Rights Abuses?

Chapter Preface   117

1. Nongovernmental Organizations Effectively Combat Human Rights Abuses   118
Robert F. Drinan

2. Nongovernmental Organizations Are Ineffective   123
Alexander Cockburn

3. Factories Should Be Required to Adhere to Minimum Standards   127
Abigail McCarthy

4. Minimum Factory Standards Will Not Prevent Human Rights Abuses   131
Medea Benjamin

5. Persecuted Women Should Be Given Political Asylum   135
Part I: *Katha Pollitt*, Part II: *Geraldine Brooks*

6. Political Asylum Should Not Be Given to All Women Claiming Persecution   141
Wayne Lutton

7. Free Trade Promotes Human Rights in China   149
James A. Dorn

8. Free Trade Does Not Promote Human Rights in China   155
Harry Wu

Periodical Bibliography   162

Chapter 4: How Should the World Respond to Crimes Against Humanity?

Chapter Preface   164

1. A Permanent International Criminal Court Should Be Created   165
Jimmy Carter

2. A Permanent International Criminal Court Would
   Be Counterproductive   169
   Bruce Fein
3. Investigating Human Cruelty May Prevent Future
   Atrocities   173
   Fred E. Katz
4. Attempts to Amend Human Rights Violations
   Will Not Alleviate Suffering   181
   Michael Ignatieff
5. The International Community Should Intervene
   on Behalf of Tibet   187
   Tenzin Gyatso
6. Chinese Rule over Tibet Should Be Accepted   194
   China Internet Information Center

Periodical Bibliography   201

For Further Discussion   202
Organizations to Contact   205
Bibliography of Books   210
Index   214

Why Consider
Opposing Viewpoints?

"The only way in which a human being can make some approach to knowing the whole of a subject is by hearing what can be said about it by persons of every variety of opinion and studying all modes in which it can be looked at by every character of mind. No wise man ever acquired his wisdom in any mode but this."

John Stuart Mill

In our media-intensive culture it is not difficult to find differing opinions. Thousands of newspapers and magazines and dozens of radio and television talk shows resound with differing points of view. The difficulty lies in deciding which opinion to agree with and which "experts" seem the most credible. The more inundated we become with differing opinions and claims, the more essential it is to hone critical reading and thinking skills to evaluate these ideas. Opposing Viewpoints books address this problem directly by presenting stimulating debates that can be used to enhance and teach these skills. The varied opinions contained in each book examine many different aspects of a single issue. While examining these conveniently edited opposing views, readers can develop critical thinking skills such as the ability to compare and contrast authors' credibility, facts, argumentation styles, use of persuasive techniques, and other stylistic tools. In short, the Opposing Viewpoints Series is an ideal way to attain the higher-level thinking and reading skills so essential in a culture of diverse and contradictory opinions.

In addition to providing a tool for critical thinking, Opposing Viewpoints books challenge readers to question their own strongly held opinions and assumptions. Most people form their opinions on the basis of upbringing, peer pressure, and personal, cultural, or professional bias. By reading carefully balanced opposing views, readers must directly confront new ideas as well as the opinions of those with whom they disagree. This is not to simplistically argue that everyone who reads opposing views will—or should—change his or her opinion. Instead, the series enhances readers' understanding of their own views by encouraging confrontation with opposing ideas. Careful examination of others' views can lead to the readers' understanding of the logical inconsistencies in their own opinions, perspective on

9

why they hold an opinion, and the consideration of the possibility that their opinion requires further evaluation.

Evaluating Other Opinions

To ensure that this type of examination occurs, Opposing Viewpoints books present all types of opinions. Prominent spokespeople on different sides of each issue as well as well-known professionals from many disciplines challenge the reader. An additional goal of the series is to provide a forum for other, less known, or even unpopular viewpoints. The opinion of an ordinary person who has had to make the decision to cut off life support from a terminally ill relative, for example, may be just as valuable and provide just as much insight as a medical ethicist's professional opinion. The editors have two additional purposes in including these less known views. One, the editors encourage readers to respect others' opinions—even when not enhanced by professional credibility. It is only by reading or listening to and objectively evaluating others' ideas that one can determine whether they are worthy of consideration. Two, the inclusion of such viewpoints encourages the important critical thinking skill of objectively evaluating an author's credentials and bias. This evaluation will illuminate an author's reasons for taking a particular stance on an issue and will aid in readers' evaluation of the author's ideas.

As series editors of the Opposing Viewpoints Series, it is our hope that these books will give readers a deeper understanding of the issues debated and an appreciation of the complexity of even seemingly simple issues when good and honest people disagree. This awareness is particularly important in a democratic society such as ours in which people enter into public debate to determine the common good. Those with whom one disagrees should not be regarded as enemies but rather as people whose views deserve careful examination and may shed light on one's own.

Thomas Jefferson once said that "difference of opinion leads to inquiry, and inquiry to truth." Jefferson, a broadly educated man, argued that "if a nation expects to be ignorant and free . . . it expects what never was and never will be." As individuals and as a nation, it is imperative that we consider the opinions of others and examine them with skill and discernment. The Opposing Viewpoints Series is intended to help readers achieve this goal.

David L. Bender & Bruno Leone,
Series Editors

Greenhaven Press anthologies primarily consist of previously published material taken from a variety of sources, including periodicals, books, scholarly journals, newspapers, government documents, and position papers from private and public organizations. These original sources are often edited for length and to ensure their accessibility for a young adult audience. The anthology editors also change the original titles of these works in order to clearly present the main thesis of each viewpoint and to explicitly indicate the opinion presented in the viewpoint. These alterations are made in consideration of both the reading and comprehension levels of a young adult audience. Every effort is made to ensure that Greenhaven Press accurately reflects the original intent of the authors included in this anthology.

INTRODUCTION

"The modern world [tends] to express moral concerns on a global scale in the language of human rights."

—Nigel Dower

To celebrate the fiftieth anniversary of the United Nations' Universal Declaration of Human Rights (UDHR), a document originally drafted in 1948, the Franklin and Eleanor Roosevelt Institute in New York City launched a Human Rights Initiative and invited concerned citizens and organizations to participate. This initiative's agenda is to encourage all nations to ratify international human rights treaties and to establish better protections for fundamental rights and freedoms. Supporters hail the initiative as a beacon of hope for people engaged in human rights struggles around the world. Others, however, question the validity of the UDHR, arguing that its claims to global relevance are belied by an overemphasis on Western ideals and values.

The concept of human rights did evolve within the Western European and North American traditions of natural rights and liberal individualism. Many historians regard the writings of seventeenth-century English philosopher John Locke as a significant early expression of the idea of natural rights. Locke argued, in effect, that nature had endowed human beings with inalienable rights that could not be usurped by any governing authority. Locke also proposed that sovereignty resided with the people rather than with the state, and that governments were obligated to protect the rights of individuals. Such ideas about rights were further articulated in two late eighteenth-century manifestos: the U.S. Bill of Rights and the French Declaration of the Rights of Man and Citizen. These documents enumerate a number of rights to which all are entitled, including the right to life, liberty, and property, the right to participate in politics and government, and the right to due process and equal protection under the law; they also establish freedom of religion, freedom of speech, and freedom of assembly. These two declarations greatly influenced political thought in the nineteenth and twentieth centuries and became models for many of the world's modern democracies.

After World War II, the newly formed United Nations drafted the Universal Declaration of Human Rights to promote respect for fundamental rights and freedoms on an international level. Borrowing heavily from previously composed democratic bills of rights, the UDHR declares the civil, political, economic, social, and cultural rights of humans—rights which are limited solely by the recognition of the rights of others and the requirements of morality and public order. In addition to the rights to life, liberty, and security of person, the UDHR lists the rights to freedom from involuntary servitude, persecution, arbitrary arrest, and torture; to freedom of thought, opinion, and expression; and to education, work, social security, rest, and a healthy standard of living. Although the UDHR is not legally binding, it is often cited as the basic human rights standard to which all nations should be held. The UDHR has also sparked the creation of international laws and treaties that call for adherence to universal standards on human rights, such as the International Covenant on Civil and Political Rights and the International Covenant on Economic, Social, and Cultural Rights.

Critics of universal human rights standards contend that such principles are not internationally applicable or enforceable. According to historian Claude E. Welck, several governments have argued that "human rights as defined in post World War II treaties . . . reflect the basic values of Western democratic, industrialized states and hence [are] not truly global." The leaders of many non-Western and third world nations assert that universal human rights standards do not reflect the needs of their populations or the social and economic agendas of their governments. A primary agenda of China's government, for example, is to maintain national and community stability by assuring that the population's basic economic and material needs are met. To this end, the government provides citizens with a free education as well as guaranteed jobs, health care, and housing. Because of these government guarantees, Chinese leaders assert, communities are made more stable: China has no homeless people, few beggars, and a very low level of crime. They contend, furthermore, that developing and maintaining a stable economy and social structure takes priority over the promotion of individual rights, such as the right to freedom of expression. Freedom of expression would actually undermine the social structure by creating community dissent and discord, Chinese authorities maintain. In the end, they argue, the individual political freedoms emphasized in the UDHR would threaten their nation's stability and economic future. They therefore implicitly reject the universal human rights standards proclaimed in the UDHR.

Critics of China's record on human rights contend that the opinions of Chinese authorities do not necessarily represent the sentiments of the Chinese people. China has resorted to the brutal suppression of prodemocracy activists and the imprisonment, torture, and execution of political dissidents who have questioned the efficacy of the socialist system or the competence of government authorities, critics point out. Human rights supporters, however, remain in a quandary over how to improve the human rights situation in China. Many activists have continued to urge the United States to impose sanctions by revoking or attaching human rights requirements to China's most-favored-nation (MFN) status. MFN affords China the same tariff treatment as other U.S. trading partners, assuring China billions of dollars from exports sold to the United States. Revoking MFN, these activists maintain, would hurt China economically and eventually force Chinese authorities to uphold internationally accepted standards on human rights. Others argue, however, that cultivating good trade relations is a better tactic for promoting human rights in China. According to James Finn, chair of the Pueblo Institute, a Catholic human rights organization, "One of the most effective ways to improve the condition of human rights in China is to increase, not diminish, trade with China." Finn and others assert that free trade promotes human rights by fostering tolerance, individual autonomy, and increased access to information. The United States has, in fact, continued normal trade relations with China, but its effects on Chinese human rights protections remain to be seen.

Undeniably, the question of achieving and enforcing universal standards on human rights is still problematic. Only nations that have ratified international human rights treaties can be held liable for human rights violations, and currently no legal apparatus allows an international organization such as the UN to usurp a nation's sovereignty in order to amend human rights violations. For these reasons, the future of human rights protections on a global level remains uncertain.

Developing and implementing universal standards on human rights is one among several topics examined in the following chapters of *Human Rights: Opposing Viewpoints*: How Should Human Rights Be Defined? What Is the State of Human Rights? What Should Be Done to Stop Human Rights Abuses? How Should the World Respond to Crimes Against Humanity? Exploring these questions reveals the competing agendas that have launched and continue to cause international debate on human rights.

CHAPTER 1

HOW SHOULD HUMAN RIGHTS BE DEFINED?

CHAPTER PREFACE

In December 1948, the United Nations adopted the Universal Declaration of Human Rights (UDHR), a thirty-article document intended to foster an international consensus on human rights and fundamental freedoms. The declaration emphasizes the equality of all individuals, proclaiming that "everyone is entitled to all the rights and freedoms" set forth in its articles. Civil and political rights are listed first, including "the right to life, liberty and security of person," freedom of opinion and expression, and the right to peaceful assembly and association. Social, economic, and cultural rights, including the right to work, rest, leisure, and education, are enumerated in the last nine articles of the document. Although declarations are not legally binding, the UDHR has often been used as a yardstick to measure governments' ability to secure rights for individuals. The UDHR's influence in the world eventually prompted negotiations that led to two international treaties: the International Covenant on Civil and Political Rights and the International Covenant on Economic, Social, and Cultural Rights, both adopted by the UN General Assembly in 1966. Governments that have ratified these covenants pledge to endorse the rights contained in the documents and to allow an elected Human Rights Committee to intervene when allegations of human rights abuses occur.

While many contend that the above documents provide a contemporary paradigm for the promotion of human rights, others argue that the ideas contained in them have a Western cultural bias and cannot be applied to many third world countries. Bilahari Kausikan, Singapore's representative to the UN, maintains that Asian societies, for example, differ from the West in their understanding of rights. He points out that while Western societies emphasize individualism and personal freedom, Asian cultures place a higher value on self-discipline and order. Thus, he asserts, while Westerners may see freedom of expression as a basic civil right, Asians may see such a right as violating the governmental authority and social order that creates national stability and economic growth. Rather than proclaiming Western values as the basis for universal human rights, the international community should foster dialogue and understanding between Asia and the West, Kausikan argues. Otherwise, he states, "it will be far more difficult to deepen and expand the international consensus on human rights."

The following chapter includes further discussion on defining human rights.

"All human rights are universal and indivisible."

HUMAN RIGHTS ARE UNIVERSAL

Pierre Sané

Some international representatives have argued that a nation's cultural values and economic needs should take precedence over the civil and political rights of its people. In the following viewpoint, Pierre Sané takes issue with this opinion, contending that basic human rights are not divisible or culturally relative. In Sané's opinion, all people deserve fundamental civil, political, and economic rights. Sané, a human rights activist from Senegal, is the secretary general of Amnesty International.

As you read, consider the following questions:

1. According to Sané, why do some nations argue that they cannot afford civil and political rights?
2. Why do some people believe that northern nations are imposing human rights standards on poverty-stricken southern nations, according to the author?
3. In Sané's opinion, what challenges has the end of the Cold War brought to the human rights community?

Reprinted from Pierre Sané, "Human Rights and the Clash of Cultures," New Perspectives Quarterly, Summer 1993, by permission of Blackwell Publishers.

The very notion of common human rights that apply to everyone and that are reinforced by an international framework that all governments should respect has been called into question. Some governments, notably from Asia, Latin America and the Middle East, have argued that a distinction of priority must be drawn between civil and political rights on the one hand and economic, social and cultural rights on the other. They contend that political and civil rights must come after economic development. Some of the poorer countries, such as Malaysia and Indonesia, argue that respect for civil and political rights is a disruptive luxury they cannot afford as they conduct the hard work of economic development. There can be no justification for this argument.

The need to feed the hungry can never mean that we should turn a blind eye to torture. Human rights are not relative. They cannot be divided or ranked. All human rights are universal and indivisible.

WEALTH SHOULD NOT DICTATE HUMAN RIGHTS STANDARDS

One of the many recent changes in world politics is the emerging tendency of the wealthier nations of Europe and America to link economic relations and the provision of humanitarian aid to a country's human rights record. This has led to the perception that human rights standards are being imposed by the North on poverty-stricken or war-torn countries of the South. This notion must also be utterly rejected.

Humanity cannot be divided into two blocs—one bloc that enjoys a measure of fundamental civil and political rights and another that can expect to be exploited and live in poverty deprived of their basic human rights.

The wealth of some nations does not give them the moral authority to dictate policies to the poorer nations.

THE CHALLENGE TO HUMAN RIGHTS

The United States recently carried out the 200th execution since reinstatement of the death penalty in the 1970s. In 1992 there was an increase in reports of torture and ill-treatment of prisoners in France, Italy, Spain and Portugal—in many cases involving a distinct element of racism. The affluent nations, including Japan and the U.S. in the case of Chinese and Haitians respectively, are subjecting asylum-seekers to unfair and summary procedures which can result in their being forced back to countries where they may face detention as prisoners of conscience, torture or death.

The challenge to human rights does not stop there. Some governments argue that the very concept of universal human rights conflicts with the culture and customs of countries influenced, for example, by Islam or Confucianism, where the bonds of community are held dearer than the needs or wishes of the individual.

EVERY GOVERNMENT'S RESPONSIBILITY

It is commonplace to say that we are in an era of profound transition, but, amidst the uncertainty, one thing remains clear: The protection of human rights is the first responsibility of every government. Indeed, the condition of human rights in a country is a good measure of the quality of its government, and the free exercise of human rights is the best safeguard against the abuse of national power.

Warren Christopher, U.S. Department of State Dispatch, May 3, 1993.

Divisions between the Islamic and non-Islamic world in particular are being exploited to promote distrust and fear. Genuine differences between conservative Islamic tradition and Western liberal societies are being misused to justify violations of rights by authoritarian regimes, such as in Saudi Arabia.

Such arguments are a transparent distraction from the real issue: These governments are committing violations that must be stopped.

CULTURAL VALUES DO NOT JUSTIFY ABUSES

No government has yet shown how the distinct values of its culture justify poverty, torture, discrimination or "disappearances."

These arguments also do not stand up to the fact that people living in the Middle East and Asia are demanding that their rights be respected. The issue is not an argument between human rights organizations and governments; it is a struggle between the people and their governments.

The end of the Cold War has further complicated the advance of human rights because ethnic and nationalist tensions have been revived on an unprecedented scale. Those movements that seek political change through armed force and the use of "ethnic cleansing" must be subject to the same arguments for the universality, indivisibility and consistency of the application of human rights as are governments.

What is at stake today is a vision of the world in which all human beings can live in the knowledge that certain basic rights are inviolable. It is the duty of each of us, individually and collectively, to see that these rights are always respected.

To this end, Amnesty International has put forward several specific proposals for improving the protection of human rights worldwide. We are calling for creation of an office of U.N. Special Commissioner for Human Rights, with the authority and resources to coordinate human rights initiatives, to integrate them into all the U.N.'s activities, and to take independent action in urgent situations such as in Bosnia-Herzegovina, Cambodia and Haiti.

We also want to see an effective U.N. "early-warning" system to identify potential human rights crises and creation of a U.N. "emergency response" system to enable the international community to react quickly to serious violations of human rights.

HUMAN RIGHTS MUST BE UNIVERSALLY RECOGNIZED

The world community must not allow divisions between North and South to be manipulated by those who try to argue that human rights are not universal—that they apply in one culture but not another; that we have to choose between countering repression and overcoming poverty.

The opening line of the U.N. Universal Declaration of Human Rights reads: "Recognition of the equal and inalienable rights of *all* members of the human family is the foundation of freedom, justice and peace in the world." These words were written more than 45 years ago. And they are as relevant in today's rapidly changing world as ever. Our stand on the universality of human rights must also remain steadfast as ever.

"Those who brew the poison of cruelty," the exiled and imprisoned Pakistani poet Faiz Ahmad Faiz, wrote, "will not win, tomorrow or today. They can put out the lamps where the lovers meet; they cannot blind the moon."

"It is simply wrong to pretend that
everything was settled . . . when the
Universal Declaration of Human
Rights was adopted."

A UNIVERSAL DEFINITION OF HUMAN RIGHTS IGNORES CULTURAL DIVERSITY

Bilahari Kausikan

Internationally defined standards on human rights often ignore cultural values, contends Bilahari Kausikan in the following viewpoint. For example, he argues, many Asians resent the emphasis that Western nations have placed on individual rights because they believe that individualism disrupts community bonds and damages a country's chances for social and economic prosperity. Instead of monopolizing the international human rights agenda, Kausikan maintains, the West should participate in a genuine human rights dialogue with Asia. Kausikan, a diplomat, represented Singapore in its negotiations at the United Nations World Conference on Human Rights held in Vienna in June 1993.

As you read, consider the following questions:

1. According to Kausikan, what was the result of the 1993 UN human rights conference in Vienna?
2. Why has Asia become more confident, in the author's opinion?
3. Which human rights abuses cannot be justified by cultural diversity, in Kausikan's opinion?

Reprinted from Bilahari Kausikan, "Human Rights Must Adjust to Asian Power," *New Perspectives Quarterly*, Fall 1993, by permission of Blackwell Publishers.

A merica and its Western allies went to the United Nations
human rights conference in Vienna in June 1993 loudly accusing a group of Asian countries of undermining the ideal of
the universality of human rights. They wanted the Vienna group
to make the strongest possible reaffirmation of this principle.
After weeks of sterile wrangling, they predictably got a diplomatic compromise that was sufficiently ambiguous to satisfy everyone, but settled nothing.

In the process, the West missed an opportunity to begin to
engage Asia in a genuine exchange on important issues. All international norms reflect a specific historical configuration of
power. As history moves on continually, every international
norm must therefore evolve through a process of debate, interpretation and reinterpretation. This is how an international consensus is built and sustained.

THE SIGNIFICANCE OF ASIAN VALUES

The economic success of much of Asia is the central strategic
fact of the 1990s. Asia's rise cannot be stopped. Power adjust-
ments are already underway which will eventually have an impact on the elaboration of international human-rights norms.

Forty-five years ago Asia was weak. Today, Asia is strong and
culturally confident because of its growing economic clout.
Most Asians do not want to be considered good Westerners,
even if they are friendly to the West. Many in Asia believe
that the West's persistent economic problems stem from what
the West cherishes as individual rights. Some suspect that attempts to foist Western interpretations of human rights on them
may be intended to drag them down to the lowest common
level.

And who is to say that they are wrong? French Prime Minister Edouard Balladur may have, perhaps inadvertently, revealed
the real reason for Western obsession with universality when he
recently accused Asians who hold "different values" of undermining France's prosperity.

Asia will insist on its own values and interests in the ongoing
interpretation of international human rights. This will require
genuine dialogue because most of Asia is now too strong to be
coerced.

THE NEED FOR A REAL DIALOGUE ON HUMAN RIGHTS

Of course, cultural diversity should not be used to shield dictators. Murder is murder whether perpetrated in America or Asia.
No nation claims torture as part of their cultural heritage.

One must keep in mind that the diversity of cultural traditions, political structures, and levels of development will make it difficult, if not impossible, to define a single distinctive and coherent human rights regime that can encompass the vast region from Japan to Burma, with its Confucian, Buddhist, Islamic, and Hindu traditions. Nonetheless, the movement toward such a goal is likely to continue. What is clear, however, is that there is general discontent throughout the region with a purely Western interpretation of human rights, and rightly so. A recent study by David Hitchcock, a former official of the United States Information Agency, showed that there are some significant differences between Asian and Western societies in the realm of values. In the Hitchcock study, Asians placed a greater value on honesty, self-discipline, and order, while Americans were more concerned about personal achievement, helping others, and personal freedom. Thus it should not surprise anyone that Asian and Western societies have different understandings of human rights and democracy.

Bilahari Kausikan, *Responsive Community*, Summer 1997.

Everyone has a right to be recognized as a person before the law. And there are other such rights that must be enjoyed by all human beings everywhere in a civilized world. But the hard core of rights that is truly universal is smaller than the West maintained at Vienna and is less enamored of unlimited individual and press freedoms. It is simply wrong to pretend that everything was settled in 1948 when the Universal Declaration of Human Rights was adopted.

WESTERN DOUBLE STANDARDS

In Vienna there was too much posturing for a real dialogue. Western double standards were exposed when the West did not support a call for action to end human-rights abuses of Bosnian Muslims. The mandate for a U.N. Human Rights Commissioner proposed by America was so unrealistic that it was opposed by the U.N. Secretary General himself. A Dutch delegate in Vienna tried to get Asian support for more money for the U.N. Center for Human Rights in a period of zero real budget growth by promising that it would not matter because his colleagues on the U.N. Budget Committee in New York would vote against the increase anyway.

Such antics contribute nothing to a real exchange on human rights. Instead, they add to the profound skepticism with which much of Asia views Western attempts to monopolize the international pulpit.

Vienna only postponed the contest between Asian and Western views on human rights that must come sooner or later. It is not impossible to reach a genuine consensus, but such a consensus will not be developed if the West denies the very need for it.

"The idea that the freedom to complain about joblessness and no medical coverage is a fundamental human right, but that jobs and health care are not, seemed ridiculous in China."

INTERNATIONAL HUMAN RIGHTS STANDARDS NEGLECT ASIAN VALUES

Robert Weil

The United States and other Western countries often claim that Asian nations—particularly China—are gross violators of human rights. Robert Weil examines this claim in the following viewpoint. While he agrees that abuses of political rights occur in China, he argues that the United States also violates human rights when it ignores poverty, police brutality, and discrimination against minorities. In Weil's opinion, the United States therefore has no credibility as the dominant defender of international human rights standards. Furthermore, he contends, the Chinese have much to contribute to the international dialogue on human rights. Weil has been an activist in the civil rights, peace, labor, environmental, and solidarity movements.

As you read, consider the following questions:

1. How did Weil's Chinese students react to the suggestion that the United States should use economic sanctions against China?
2. According to the author, what would the Chinese like to include as part of a human rights agenda?
3. In Weil's opinion, what is the one "human right" that the U.S. government has consistently upheld?

Reprinted from Robert Weil, "Of Human Rights and Wrongs: China and the United States," *Monthly Review*, July/August 1994, by permission of Monthly Review Foundation. Copyright ©1994 by Monthly Review Inc.

The March 1994 visit of [former] Secretary of State Warren Christopher to Beijing, calling on the Chinese government to improve its human rights record under the threat of denying it renewal of Most Favored Nation trade status, ended in fiasco. It should hardly have come as a surprise. After a semester teaching at a university and a month travelling in China, the attitudes and conditions I observed make clear why the U.S. human rights policy toward that nation was virtually certain to be rejected. Conversations with Chinese, most of whom were students, showed that the effort of the U.S. government to act as the enforcer of universal standards in their country is meeting not only with official rejection, but with very strong popular opposition. An understanding of this reaction requires altering the perspective from which the issue is commonly approached in the United States, and questioning the very definition of human rights that prevails here. To do so reveals that the United States has as much to learn from the Chinese in this area, as vice versa. These "lessons" for the United States in regard to human rights are similar to the ones being voiced across Asia, from Japan to Singapore. But in China, they also draw on the experience of decades of socialist revolution.

No Support for Sanctions Against China

The 150 or so graduate students that my wife and I taught were from the very "Tiananmen generation" that filled U.S. television screens with their anti-government protests in 1989, ending in the terrible events of June 3 and 4 and the continuing repression of dissidents down to today. These young people keenly felt the restrictions placed on their ability to communicate freely and to influence the policies of their country. It was all the more striking, therefore, that among these students support for the Chinese government in its showdown with the United States over human rights was both widespread and intense. In our many discussions of this issue both inside and outside class, not a single student voiced anything but opposition—often with great anger—to the prospect of the United States applying economic sanctions to China. Indeed, it was on this subject, more than once, that the most passive and seemingly apolitical students, or those most attracted to Western culture, suddenly spoke up forcefully. Given this indication of popular backing of official policy among the very group where it might be expected to be weakest, it was virtually a given that China would stonewall the United States on this issue.

To understand the apparent anomalies of this situation, it is necessary to look carefully at the Chinese attitude on human rights, especially in relation to the United States and the world community. Most treatments of this question in the U.S. media, paralleled by the stand of leading organizations active in this area, simply parrot the administration position that the Chinese government is a major violator of international standards, with the only debate being over which forms of pressure are most appropriate and likely to bring about necessary changes. This view assumes that the United States stands for universal values, and that it has the right to serve as their global enforcer in China. By extension, much is made of the supposed "conflict" between the U.S. government and certain multinational corporations, who are said to put business interests above the need for human rights in dealing with the Chinese. That the United States might actually have something positive to learn from China on this issue does not even arise for those who start from this perspective.

HUMAN RIGHTS CONCERNS IN CHINA

The occasional effort to be sensitive to opposing Chinese attitudes on human rights usually takes the form of noting that China does not have a history of western-style political democracy and individual liberties. But this still leaves China defined in essentially negative terms, as simply lacking what we have. Even more infrequently, mention is made of the Chinese assertion that national sovereignty and economic justice must also be part of the human rights agenda, but these are almost never explored in depth, the implication being left that they are of lesser value, and perhaps advanced by the Chinese government only as a cover, to deflect attention from its problems with "real" human rights. The corollary, sometimes stated openly, at other times implied, is that the U.S. quarrel is only with the authorities in Beijing, it being assumed that the people of China share opposition to their government on this issue and would welcome intervention from outside.

Our Chinese students did indeed voice human rights complaints, the most frequent of which concerned the lack of greater freedom of speech and of a non-governmental press. They were clearly distressed that there were no regular channels through which government policies could be openly criticized, much less changed. In all probability, these concerns overlay even deeper fears that were not necessarily exposed to us as temporary foreign visitors. But these students nevertheless offered strong support for the three primary objections raised by the government of China to the attempt of the United States to impose its human rights conception on others.

U.S. HYPOCRISY ON HUMAN RIGHTS

First is the problem of a double standard. Leaving aside U.S. creation of and support for some of the worst violators of human rights in the world, such as the Guatemalan military regime, the Chinese question the practices of the United States itself. Tiananmen? How about Panama City six months later? Tibet? What about Puerto Rico? Refusal to accept universal international standards? But the United States itself stonewalled the World Court ruling to pay reparations to Nicaragua. Police repression? All our students had seen Rodney King beaten on TV and the widespread destruction that followed. Political dissidents? A short list for the United States would have to include Leonard Peltier, Puerto Rican *independentistas*, and the black victims of COINTELPRO [the FBI's Counterintelligence Program of the 1960s] imprisoned, murdered, or driven into exile. Prison labor? While we were in China, the press was reporting on the growing U.S. export of goods produced by prisoners. None of these parallels are exact, and any given student was usually familiar with only some of them. But all knew enough about these and other similar situations that, whatever their own attitude toward Chinese human rights, they believed strongly that the United States comes with filthy hands, hypocrisy and arrogance to the role of global enforcer in their country.

China also insists that national sovereignty is just as much an issue of human rights as are individual liberties. Thus the very attempt of the United States to impose its will on the Chinese is seen as violating their human right to self-determination. As an immensely old and proud culture, now attempting to regain its position as a global leader, China sees the current human rights pressure from the West as just one more attempt to "civilize" the Chinese, right in line with the missionaries, opium, and gunboats of old. Thus our students were deeply suspicious that human rights too is being used as an imperialist weapon to keep China down. They put it in the same category as the denial of the Chinese Olympic bid, and the sudden last-minute passion of the Hong Kong authorities for "democracy" after 150 years of appointed colonial government and just three years before reversion to China. Citing such conflicts as the "Yinhe" freighter incident in the fall of 1993 in which the United States falsely claimed the Chinese were shipping military chemicals to Iran, many spoke bitterly of the self-appointed role of the United

America's cup.

States as "global policeman."

But the most critical issue, and the one most relevant to progressives and the left in the United States, is the basic question of what kind of "human rights" are considered universal standards. We lived in a northeast Chinese industrial and university city of 2 million people, only now beginning to feel the full effects of the "marketization" policies of the government. Still, following earlier socialist principles, workers in the local auto factories were paid approximately twice as much as most of the faculty at our school. Despite a very low general economic level there were no homeless, and in four and a half months, we saw two people with physical problems begging at the local temple, and what seemed like a single "bag lady." When the weather turned bitter cold, a couple more adult beggars showed up in the downtown tunnels. But we never saw a single child beg, or so much as ask a stranger for candy or chewing gum. There was practically no crime, and women walked freely alone at night. Having lived in and around New York City, I was particularly struck by the way people moved down the generally dark streets without checking out who was approaching them, even from behind. Our students enjoyed a virtually free education, including at the graduate level, and looked forward to guaranteed jobs, with health care and housing, remnants of the socialist system. Indeed about half of them came directly to the university from work units.

Despite the emphasis in the United States on governmental domination of China, we began to feel there what "civil" society means. For those living and working in such an environment, the idea that a vastly wealthy country like the United States, with several dozen billionaires, but in which millions are unemployed and without health insurance and hundreds of thousands live homeless on the streets, where teenagers routinely murder each other and bystanders with automatic weapons fighting over drugs, and even children carry guns to primary school, where the rate of incarceration is higher than in South Africa [under apartheid] and there are 2,500 on death row, but crime is so rampant that entire communities cower at night behind security devices and strangers are shot just for knocking on the wrong door, where women have to try to "take back the night" . . . that such a country can serve as the global enforcer of universal human rights seemed simply ludicrous.

HUMAN RIGHTS TRADEOFFS

For these students, what was hardest of all to understand was why African-Americans and Latinos have to periodically burn down the centers of major cities to call attention to their never-ending oppression and poverty. Over and over, I was asked why the U.S. government does not do something to end these conditions. While their own view of the Chinese treatment of minority nationalities was undoubtedly too rosy, their attitudes at least reflected the official line that the non-Han peoples are equals and that their regions should receive special economic advantages on the road to development. Raised in a system with a socialist conception of governmental activism and a media that constantly presents positive images of minorities, the idea that any society would allow a problem like the U.S. "inner cities" to fester endlessly without any serious attempt to address it on the national level was beyond their ken.

In trying to explain this gap in social perception and policy, my most effective method was to read them the New York Times article from a few years back concerning a court ruling that the homeless in Grand Central Station had the right to beg, but only because they were protected under the free speech provisions of the First Amendment. As it turned out, even this freedom proved less sacrosanct than the right of corporate commuters not to have to look into the faces of the human wreckage the U.S. capitalist system produces, and the decision was soon reversed. My students, nevertheless, got the point: that in the United States there is no human rights guarantee against starvation, homelessness, unemployment, or lack of health care, only the political freedom to protest—sometimes—that one is starving, homeless, jobless, or dying. As much as they themselves yearned for greater freedom to speak, write, and complain freely, the U.S. "tradeoff" of political for economic rights did not strike these students as particularly attractive, and it certainly did not represent for them a standard of universal justice.

In this same vein, when I once remarked to one of my classes that I felt much freer talking openly about socialist concepts with them than I ever had in a classroom in the United States, one student replied, only half-jokingly: "At least in China, we can discuss both socialism and capitalism." Still, many of them made clear that they envied the human right to speak relatively more freely that, as a U.S. citizen, they believed I enjoyed. I assured them that, having accepted the teaching position in China in large measure because I lacked regular employment and adequate health coverage for myself and my family in the United States, and that I would soon return to the same conditions (as indeed I have), the envy flowed both ways. The idea that the freedom to complain about joblessness and no medical coverage is a fundamental human right, but that jobs and health care are not, seemed ridiculous in China.

ON THE RIGHT TO ECONOMIC DEVELOPMENT

Our students, like the Chinese government, raised a fourth aspect of human rights in arguing against the U.S. position, perhaps the most crucial of all in their eyes at the present time. This is the right of Third World countries to rise from the poverty and subordination to which the imperialist economic system has consigned them. For the Chinese, this has become an overriding goal, in the pursuit of which other rights can and must for now be restricted. They speak of greater political democratization emerging in time from an expanding economy, in a mirror image of the United States claim that all economic problems can ultimately be solved through the normal channels of politics. Both positions may be equally specious. But there is no fundamental reason why either claim should be privileged over the other as a basis for global human rights standards, and China refuses to recognize any such arbitrary assertion. Any idea that the rapidly expanding economy might have to be slowed down to accommodate political democratization did not have much appeal, and attempts to enforce such a view from outside were once again met by our students with suspicion that they are only meant to hold China back. . . .

The only "human right" which either the U.S. government or business community has ever consistently fought for is the freedom for some to make capitalist profit off the exploitation and misery of others. Toward this end there is no violation of human rights they have not been willing to commit or condone, no democratically-elected government they have not been prepared to overthrow, no socialist society they have not striven to destroy. Only when it fits this larger agenda does the issue of political freedom and civil liberties get raised, and only very selectively at that. Perfectly expressing this relation, a "compromise" position has now been floated by the Clinton administration and some in Congress, and backed by exiled dissidents such as Fang Lizhi, in which only state-owned enterprises in China would be subject to trade sanctions, to "'encourage the private sector'. . . and reduce the impact on American business and on places like Hong Kong and Taiwan" (*New York Times*, March 30, 1994, p. A10). Given the hypocrisy and cynicism of this approach, it is hardly wild speculation to suggest that, should China become fully capitalistic, "human rights" of any kind there would rapidly disappear as a United States concern.

THE CHINESE DESERVE RESPECT

Faced with such a choice of U.S. "friends," many Chinese adopt a "curse on all your houses" stand. They are concerned with making their own society, which today at least is still officially "socialist," work better. This certainly includes developing new forms of democratic expression and decision-making. But there is no reason to believe that the best forms of the latter for China are those which were developed in parallel with Western capitalism. As that country knows only too well, any attempt to achieve the simultaneous implementation of human rights in the areas of political freedoms, economic development, and social justice is extremely difficult. The Chinese have had as much and as painful experience with these interlocking struggles as any people on the globe. It behooves the rest of the world, including the United States, to approach them with an attitude of respect and humility, and in the posture of student as much as teacher.

"The claim to 'Asian values' hardly constitutes a serious threat to the universal validity of human rights."

INTERNATIONAL HUMAN RIGHTS STANDARDS ARE RELEVANT TO ASIAN SOCIETIES

Xiaorong Li

Many have argued that Asian countries have a unique perspective on human rights that is generally not represented in the international human rights agenda. Asian values, they contend, dictate that community, social, and economic rights should take priority over individual, civil, and political rights. In the following viewpoint, Xiaorong Li disagrees with this argument. Maintaining that Asian values are more varied and complex than is typically claimed, Li asserts that international standards on human rights—even if of Western origin—are relevant to Asian societies. Moreover, Li concludes, universal standards on human rights are possible despite differences among cultures. Li is a research scholar for the Institute for Philosophy and Public Policy at the University of Maryland in College Park.

As you read, consider the following questions:
1. According to Li, what four claims constitute the so-called "Asian view" of human rights?
2. In the author's opinion, why should leaders who place economic development rights over political rights be viewed with suspicion?
3. In what three ways can a value be universal or culturally specific, according to Li?

Reprinted from Xiaorong Li, "'Asian Values' and the Universality of Human Rights," *Report from the Institute for Philosophy and Public Policy*, Spring 1996, by permission.

Orientalist scholarship in the nineteenth century perceived Asians as the mysterious and backward people of the Far East. Ironically, as this century draws to a close, leaders of prosperous and entrepreneurial East and Southeast Asian countries eagerly stress Asia's incommensurable differences from the West and demand special treatment of their human rights record by the international community. They reject outright the globalization of human rights and claim that Asia has a unique set of values, which, as Singapore's ambassador to the United Nations has urged, provide the basis for Asia's different understanding of human rights and justify the "exceptional" handling of rights by Asian governments.

Is this assertion of "Asian values" simply a cloak for arrogant regimes whose newly gained confidence from rapidly growing economic power makes them all the more resistant to outside criticism? Does it have any intellectual substance? What challenges has the "Asian values" debate posed to a human rights movement committed to globalism?

Though scholars have explored the understanding of human rights in various Asian contexts, the concept of "Asian values" gains political prominence only when it is articulated in government rhetoric and official statements. In asserting these values, leaders from the region find that they have a convenient tool to silence internal criticism and to fan anti-Western nationalist sentiments. At the same time, the concept is welcomed by cultural relativists, cultural supremacists, and isolationists alike, as fresh evidence for their various positions against a political liberalism that defends universal human rights and democracy. Thus, the "Asian values" debate provides an occasion to reinvigorate deliberation about the foundations of human rights, the sources of political legitimacy, and the relation between modernity and cultural identity.

This essay makes a preliminary attempt to identify the myths, misconceptions, and fallacies that have gone into creating an "Asian view" of human rights. By sorting out the various threads in the notions of "cultural specificity" and "universality," it shows that the claim to "Asian values" hardly constitutes a serious threat to the universal validity of human rights.

DEFINING THE "ASIAN VIEW"

To speak of an "Asian view" of human rights that has supposedly emanated from Asian perspectives or values is itself problematic: it is impossible to defend the "Asianness" of this view and its legitimacy in representing Asian culture(s). "Asia" in our ordinary language designates large geographic areas which house diverse political entities (states) and their people, with drastically different cultures and religions, and unevenly developed (or undeveloped) economies and political systems. Those who assert commonly shared "Asian values" cannot reconcile their claims with the immense diversity of Asia—a heterogeneity that extends to its people, their social-political practices and ethnic-cultural identities. Nonetheless, official statements by governments in the region typically make the following claims about the so-called "Asian view" of human rights:

Claim I: Rights are "culturally specific." Human rights emerge in the context of particular social, economic, cultural and political conditions. The circumstances that prompted the institutionalization of human rights in the West do not exist in Asia. China's 1991 White Paper stated that "[o]wing to tremendous differences in historical background, social system, cultural tradition and economic development, countries differ in their understanding and practice of human rights." In the Bangkok Governmental Declaration, endorsed at the 1993 Asian regional preparatory meeting for the Vienna World Conference on Human Rights, governments agreed that human rights "must be considered in the context of a dynamic and evolving process of international norm-setting, bearing in mind the significance of national and regional peculiarities and various historical, cultural, and religious backgrounds."

COMMUNITY RIGHTS VERSUS INDIVIDUAL RIGHTS

Claim II: The community takes precedence over individuals. The importance of the community in Asian culture is incompatible with the primacy of the individual, upon which the Western notion of human rights rests. The relationship between individuals and communities constitutes the key difference between Asian and Western cultural "values." An official statement of the Singapore government, Shared Values (1991), stated that "[a]n emphasis on the community has been a key survival value for Singapore." Human rights and the rule of law, according to the "Asian view," are individualistic by nature and hence destructive of Asia's social mechanism. Increasing rates of violent crime, family breakdown, homelessness, and drug abuse are cited as evidence that Western individualism (particularly the American variety) has failed.

Claim III: Social and economic rights take precedence over civil and political rights. Asian societies rank social and economic rights and "the right to economic development" over individuals' political and

35

civil rights. The Chinese White Paper (1991) stated that "[t]o eat their fill and dress warmly were the fundamental demands of the Chinese people who had long suffered cold and hunger." Political and civil rights, on this view, do not make sense to poor and illiterate multitudes; such rights are not meaningful under destitute and unstable conditions. The right of workers to form independent unions, for example, is not as urgent as stability and efficient production. Implicit here is the promise that once people's basic needs are met—once they are adequately fed, clothed, and educated—and the social order is stable, the luxury of civil and political rights will be extended to them. In the meantime, economic development will be achieved more efficiently if the leaders are authorized to restrict individuals' political and civil rights for the sake of political stability.

Claim IV: Rights are a matter of national sovereignty. The right of a nation to self-determination includes a government's domestic jurisdiction over human rights. Human rights are internal affairs, not to be interfered with by foreign states or multinational agencies. In its 1991 White Paper, China stated that "the issue of human rights falls by and large within the sovereignty of each state." In 1995, the Chinese government confirmed its opposition to "some countries' hegemonic acts of using a double standard for the human rights of other countries . . . and imposing their own pattern on others, or interfering in the internal affairs of other countries by using 'human rights' as a pretext." The West's attempt to apply universal standards of human rights to developing countries is disguised cultural imperialism and an attempt to obstruct their development.

ARE RIGHTS "CULTURALLY SPECIFIC"?

In this essay I address the first three claims that make up the "Asian view," particularly the argument that rights are "culturally specific." This argument implies that social norms originating in other cultures should not be adopted in Asian culture. But, in practice, advocates of the "Asian view" often do not consistently adhere to this rule. Leaders from the region pick and choose freely from other cultures, adopting whatever is in their political interest. They seem to have no qualms about embracing such things as capitalist markets and consumerist culture. What troubles them about the concept of human rights, then, turns out to have little to do with its Western cultural origin.

In any case, there are no grounds for believing that norms originating *elsewhere* should be inherently unsuitable for solving problems *here.* Such a belief commits the "genetic fallacy" in that it assumes that a norm is suitable only to the culture of its origin. But the origin of an idea in one culture does not entail its unsuitability to another culture. If, for example, there are good reasons for protecting the free expression of Asian people, free expression should be respected, no matter whether the idea of free expression originated in the West or Asia, or how long it has been a viable idea. And in fact, Asian countries may have now entered into historical circumstances where the affirmation and protection of human rights is not only possible but desirable.

Look! Development!

Reprinted from the *Sri Lanka Human Rights Bulletin*, April 1986. Courtesy of the *Bulletin of Concerned Asian Scholars*.

In some contemporary Asian societies, we find economic, social, cultural, and political conditions that foster demands for human rights as the norm-setting criteria for the treatment of individual persons and the communities they form. National aggregate growth and distribution, often under the control of authoritarian governments, have not benefited individuals from vulnerable social groups—including workers, women, children, and indigenous or minority populations. Social and economic disparities are rapidly expanding. Newly introduced market forces, in the absence of rights protection and the rule of law, have further exploited and disadvantaged these groups and created anxiety even among more privileged sectors—professionals and business owners, as well as foreign corporations—in places where corruption, disrespect for property rights, and arbitrary rule are the norm. Political dissidents, intellectuals and opposition groups who dare to challenge the system face persecution. Meanwhile, with the expansion of communications technology and improvements in literacy, information about repression and injustice has become more accessible both within and beyond previously isolated communities; it is increasingly known that the notion of universal rights has been embraced by people in many Latin American, African, and some East and Southeast Asian countries (Japan, South Korea, Taiwan, and the Philippines). Finally, the international human rights movement has developed robust non-Western notions of human rights, including economic, social, and cultural rights, providing individuals in Asia with powerful tools to fight against poverty, corruption, military repression, discrimination, cultural and community destruction, as well as social, ethnic, and religious violence. Together, these new circumstances make human rights relevant and implementable in Asian societies.

CULTURE, COMMUNITY, AND THE STATE

The second claim, that Asians value community over individuality, obscures more than it reveals about community, its relations to the state and individuals, and the conditions congenial to its flourishing. The so-called Asian value of "community harmony" is used as an illustration of "cultural" differences between Asian and Western societies, in order to show that the idea of individuals' inalienable rights does not suit Asian societies. This "Asian communitarianism" is a direct challenge to what is perceived as the essence of human rights, i.e., its individual-centered approach, and it suggests that Asia's community-centered approach is superior.

However, the "Asian view" creates confusions by collapsing "community" into the state and the state into the (current) regime. When equations are drawn between community, the state and the regime, any criticisms of the regime become crimes against the nation-state, the community, and the people. The "Asian view" relies on such a conceptual maneuver to dismiss individual rights that conflict with the regime's interest, allowing the condemnation of individual rights as anti-communal, destructive of social harmony, and seditionist against the sovereign state.

At the same time, this view denies the existence of conflicting interests between the state (understood as a political entity) and communities (understood as voluntary, civil associations) in Asian societies. What begins as an endorsement of the value of community and social harmony ends in an assertion of the supreme status of the regime and its leaders. Such a regime is capable of dissolving any non-governmental organizations it dislikes in the name of "community interest," often citing traditional Confucian values of social harmony to defend restrictions on the right to free association and expression, and thus wields ever more pervasive control over unorganized individual workers and dissenters. A Confucian communitarian, however, would find that the bleak, homogeneous society that these governments try to shape through draconian practices—criminal prosecutions for "counterrevolutionary activities," administrative detention, censorship, and military curfew—has little in common with her ideal of social harmony.

Contrary to the "Asian view," individual freedom is not intrinsically opposed to and destructive of community. Free association, free expression, and tolerance are vital to the well-being of communities. Through open public deliberations, marginalized and vulnerable social groups can voice their concerns and expose the discrimination and unfair treatment they encounter. In a liberal democratic society, which is mocked and denounced by some Asian leaders for its individualist excess, a degree of separation between the state and civil society provides a public space for the flourishing of communities.

A FALSE DILEMMA

The third claim of the "Asian view," that economic development rights have a priority over political and civil rights, supposes that the starving and illiterate masses have to choose between starvation and oppression. It then concludes that "a full belly" would no doubt be the natural choice. Setting aside the paternalism of this assumption, the question arises of whether the apparent trade-off—freedom in exchange for food—actually brings an end to deprivation, and whether people must in fact choose between these two miserable states of affairs.

When it is authoritarian leaders who pose this dilemma, one should be particularly suspicious. The oppressors, after all, are well-positioned to amass wealth for themselves, and their declared project of enabling people to "get rich" may increase the disparity between the haves and the have-nots. Moreover, the most immediate victims of oppression—those subjected to imprisonment or torture—are often those who have spoken out against the errors or the incompetence of authorities who have failed to alleviate deprivation, or who in fact have made it worse. The sad truth is that an authoritarian regime can practice political repression and starve the poor at the same time. Conversely, an end to oppression often means the alleviation of poverty—as when, to borrow Amartya Sen's example, accountable governments manage to avert famine by heeding the warnings of a free press.

Is Economic Development a Human Right?

One assumption behind this false dilemma is that "the right to development" is a state's sovereign right and that it is one and the same as the "social-economic rights" assigned to individuals under international covenants. But the right of individuals and communities to participate in and enjoy the fruit of economic development should not be identified with the right of nation-states to pursue national pro-development policies, even if such policies set the stage for individual citizens to exercise their economic rights. Even when "the right to development" is understood as a sovereign state right, as is sometimes implied in the international politics of development, it belongs to a separate and distinct realm from that of "social-economic rights."

The distinction between economic rights and the state's right to development goes beyond the issue of who holds these particular rights. National development is an altogether different matter from securing the economic rights of vulnerable members of society. National economic growth does not guarantee that basic subsistence for the poor will be secured. While the right to development (narrowly understood) enables the nation-state as a unit to grow economically, social-economic rights are concerned with empowering the poor and vulnerable, preventing their marginalization and exploitation, and securing their basic subsistence. What the right of development, when asserted by an authoritarian state, tends to disregard, but what social-economic rights aspire to protect, is fair economic equality or social equity. Unfortunately, Asia's development programs have not particularly enabled the poor and vulnerable to control their basic livelihood, especially where development is narrowly understood as the creation of markets and measured by national aggregate growth rates.

A more plausible argument for ranking social and economic rights above political and civil rights is that poor and illiterate people cannot really exercise their civil-political rights. Yet the poor and illiterate may benefit from civil and political freedom by speaking, without fear, of their discontent. Meanwhile, as we have seen, political repression does not guarantee better living conditions and education for the poor and illiterate. The leaders who are in a position to encroach upon citizens' rights to express political opinions will also be beyond reproach and accountability for failures to protect citizens' social-economic rights.

Political-civil rights and social-economic-cultural rights are in many ways indivisible. Each is indispensable for the effective exercise of the other. If citizens' civil-political rights are unprotected, their opportunities to "get rich" can be taken away just as arbitrarily as they are bestowed; if citizens have no real opportunity to exercise their social-economic rights, their rights to political participation and free expression will be severely undermined. For centuries, poverty has stripped away the human dignity of Asia's poor masses, making them vulnerable to violations of their cultural and civil-political rights. Today, a free press and the rule of law are likely to enhance Asians' economic opportunity. Political-civil rights are not a mere luxury of rich nations, as some Asian leaders have told their people, but a safety net for marginalized and vulnerable people in dramatically changing Asian societies.

UNIVERSALITY VERSUS CULTURAL SPECIFICITY

The threat posed by "Asian values" to the universality of human rights seems ominous. If Asian cultural relativism prevails, there can be no universal standards to adjudicate between competing conceptions of human rights. But one may pause and ask whether the "Asian values" debate has created any really troubling threat to universal human rights—that is, serious enough to justify the alarm that it has touched off.

The answer, I argue, depends on how one understands the concepts of universality and cultural specificity. In essence, there are three ways in which a value can be universal or culturally specific. First, these terms may refer to the *origin* of a value. In this sense, they represent a claim about whether a value has developed only within specific cultures, or whether it has arisen within the basic ideas of every culture.

No one on either side of the "Asian values" debate thinks that human rights are universal with respect to their origin. It is accepted that the idea of human rights originated in Western traditions. The universalist does not disagree with the cultural relativist on this point—though they would disagree about its significance—and it is not in this sense that human rights are understood as having universality.

Second, a value may be culturally specific or universal with respect to its prospects for *effective (immediate) implementation*. That is, a value may find favorable conditions for its implementation only within certain cultures, or it may find such conditions everywhere in the world.

Now, I don't think that the universalist would insist that human rights can be immediately or effectively implemented in all societies, given their vastly different conditions. No one imagines that human rights will be fully protected in societies that are ravaged by violent conflict or warfare; where political power is so unevenly distributed that the ruling forces can crush any opposition; where social mobility is impossible, and people segregated by class, caste system, or cultural taboos are isolated and uninformed; where most people are on the verge of starvation and where survival is the pressing concern. The list could go on. However, to acknowledge that the prospects for effective implementation of human rights differ according to circumstances is not to legitimize violations under these unfavorable conditions, nor is it to deny the universal applicability or validity of human rights (as defined below) to all human beings no matter what circumstances they face.

A CROSS-CULTURAL CONVERSATION ON HUMAN RIGHTS

Third, a value may be understood as culturally specific by people who think it is *valid* only within certain cultures. According to this understanding, a value can be explained or defended only by appealing to assumptions already accepted by a given culture; in cultures that do not share those assumptions, the validity of such a value will become questionable. Since there are few universally shared cultural assumptions that can be invoked in defense of the concept of human rights, the universal validity of human rights is problematic.

The proponents of this view suppose that the validity of human rights can only be assessed in an intracultural conversation where certain beliefs or assumptions are commonly shared and not open to scrutiny. However, an intercultural conversation about the validity of human rights is now taking place among people with different cultural assumptions; it is a conversation that proceeds by opening those assumptions to reflection and reexamination. Its participants begin with some minimal shared beliefs: for example, that genocide, slavery, and racism are wrong. They accept some basic rules of argumentation to reveal hidden presuppositions, disclose inconsistencies between ideas, clarify conceptual ambiguity and confusions, and expose conclusions based on insufficient evidence and oversimplified generalizations. In such a conversation based on public reasoning, people may come to agree on a greater range of issues than seemed possible when they began. They may revise or reinterpret their old beliefs. The plausibility of such a conversation suggests a way of establishing universal validity: that is, by referring to public reason in defense of a particular conception or value.

If the concept of human rights can survive the scrutiny of public reason in such a cross-cultural conversation, its universal validity will be confirmed. An idea that has survived the test of rigorous scrutiny will be reasonable or valid not just within the boundaries of particular cultures, but reasonable in a non-relativistic fashion. The deliberation and public reasoning will continue, and it may always be possible for the concept of human rights to become doubtful and subject to revision. But the best available public reasons so far seem to support its universal validity. Such public reasons include the arguments against genocide, slavery, and racial discrimination. Others have emerged from the kind of reasoning that reveals fallacies, confusions, and mistakes involved in the defense of Asian cultural exceptionalism.

"Women will never gain full dignity until their human rights are respected and protected."

A HUMAN RIGHTS AGENDA MUST INCLUDE WOMEN'S RIGHTS

Hillary Rodham Clinton

In the following viewpoint, Hillary Rodham Clinton maintains that women's rights must become a part of the international human rights agenda. She points out that women all over the world continue to face myriad abuses, including poverty, sex discrimination, forced prostitution, rape, genital mutilation, and domestic violence. These atrocities against women must be recognized as human rights violations, Clinton argues. Clinton, who became First Lady of the United States in 1993, is an attorney who has worked to improve child welfare and to enact health care reform. This viewpoint was originally delivered as a speech at the United Nations Fourth World Conference on Women in Beijing, China, on September 5, 1995.

As you read, consider the following questions:

1. In the author's opinion, what are the most important issues in women's lives?
2. What percentage of the world's poor do women comprise, according to Clinton?
3. What challenges do American women face, in Clinton's opinion?

Reprinted from Hillary Rodham Clinton's speech, "When Communities Flourish," Beijing, China, September 5, 1995.

I would like to thank the Secretary General of the United Nations for inviting me to be part of the United Nations Fourth World Conference on Women. This is truly a celebration—a celebration of the contributions women make in every aspect of life: in the home, on the job, in their communities, as mothers, wives, sisters, daughters, learners, workers, citizens and leaders.

It is also a coming together, much the way women come together every day in every country.

We come together in fields and in factories. In village markets and supermarkets. In living rooms and board rooms.

Whether it is while playing with our children in the park, or washing clothes in a river, or taking a break at the office water cooler, we come together and talk about our aspirations and concerns. And time and again, our talk turns to our children and our families. However different we may be, there is far more that unites us than divides us. We share a common future. And we are here to find common ground so that we may help bring new dignity and respect to women and girls all over the world—and in so doing, bring new strength and stability to families as well.

WHAT MATTERS MOST TO WOMEN

By gathering in Beijing, we are focusing world attention on issues that matter most in the lives of women and their families: access to education, health care, jobs and credit, the chance to enjoy basic legal and human rights and participate fully in the political life of their countries.

There are some who question the reason for this conference.

Let them listen to the voices of women in their homes, neighborhoods, and workplaces.

There are some who wonder whether the lives of women and girls matter to economic and political progress around the globe.

Let them look at the women gathered here and at Huairou—the homemakers, nurses, teachers, lawyers, policymakers, and women who run their own businesses.

It is conferences like this that compel governments and people everywhere to listen, look and face the world's most pressing problems.

Wasn't it after the women's conference in Nairobi [in 1985] that the world focused for the first time on the crisis of domestic violence?

Earlier today [September 5, 1995], I participated in a World Health Organization forum, where government officials, NGOs [nongovernmental organizations], and individual citizens are working on ways to address the health problems of women and girls.

Tomorrow [September 6, 1995], I will attend a gathering of the United Nations Development Fund for Women. There, the discussion will focus on local—and highly successful—programs that give hard-working women access to credit so they can improve their own lives and the lives of their families.

What we are learning around the world is that if women are healthy and educated, their families will flourish. If women are free from violence, their families will flourish. If women have a chance to work and earn as full and equal partners in society, their families will flourish.

And when families flourish, communities and nations will flourish.

That is why every woman, every man, every child, every family, and every nation on our planet has a stake in the discussion that takes place here.

The Challenges Facing Women

Over the past 25 years, I have worked persistently on issues relating to women, children and families. I have had the opportunity to learn more about the challenges facing women in my own country and around the world.

I have met new mothers in Jojakarta, Indonesia, who come together regularly in their village to discuss nutrition, family planning, and baby care.

I have met working parents in Denmark who talk about the comfort they feel in knowing that their children can be cared for in creative, safe, and nurturing after-school centers.

I have met women in South Africa who helped lead the struggle to end apartheid and are now helping build a new democracy.

I have met with the leading women of the Western Hemisphere who are working every day to promote literacy and better health care for the children of their countries.

I have met women in India and Bangladesh who are taking out small loans to buy milk cows, rickshaws, thread and other materials to create a livelihood for themselves and their families.

I have met doctors and nurses in Belarus and Ukraine who are trying to keep children alive in the aftermath of Chernobyl.

The great challenge of this Conference is to give voice to women everywhere whose experiences go unnoticed, whose words go unheard.

Women comprise more than half the world's population. Women are 70 percent of the world's poor, and two-thirds of those who are not taught to read and write.

Women are the primary caretakers for most of the world's children and elderly. Yet much of the work we do is not valued—not by economists, not by historians, not by popular culture, not by government leaders.

At this very moment, as we sit here, women around the world are giving birth, raising children, cooking meals, washing clothes, cleaning houses, planting crops, working on assembly lines, running companies, and running countries.

Women also are dying from diseases that should have been prevented or treated; they are watching their children succumb to malnutrition caused by poverty and economic deprivation; they are being denied the right to go to school by their own fathers and brothers; they are being forced into prostitution, and they are being barred from the bank lending office and banned from the ballot box.

THE HUMAN RIGHTS OF WOMEN

The most significant development at the United Nations' Fourth World Conference on Women, held in Beijing in September 1995, may well be the one that has received the least comment. Midway through what sometimes seemed like endless round-the-clock negotiations, a working session finally agreed to recognize that the human rights of women include the right to exercise control over their own sexuality—free of coercion, discrimination, and violence.

With this consensus, the vast majority of the world's governments acknowledged that previous guarantees of political and economic equality remain hollow so long as women are unprotected from physical violation and sexual abuse in the home and outside of it.

Ellen Chesler and Joan Dunlop, *Christian Science Monitor*, September 29, 1995.

Those of us who have the opportunity to be here have the responsibility to speak for those who could not.

As an American, I want to speak up for women in my own country—women who are raising children on the minimum wage, women who can't afford health care or child care, women whose lives are threatened by violence, including violence in their own homes.

I want to speak up for mothers who are fighting for good schools, safe neighborhoods, clean air and clean airwaves; for older women, some of them widows, who have raised their families and now find that their skills and life experiences are not valued in the workplace; for women who are working all night as nurses, hotel clerks, and fast food cooks so that they can be at home during the day with their kids; and for women everywhere who simply don't have time to do everything they are called upon to do each day.

Speaking to you today, I speak for them, just as each of us speaks for women around the world who are denied the chance to go to school, or see a doctor, or own property, or have a say about the direction of their lives, simply because they are women. The truth is that most women around the world work both inside and outside the home, usually by necessity.

RESPECTING WOMEN'S CHOICES

We need to understand that there is no formula for how women should lead their lives.

That is why we must respect the choices that each woman makes for herself and her family. Every woman deserves the chance to realize her God-given potential.

We also must recognize that women will never gain full dignity until their human rights are respected and protected.

Our goals for this Conference, to strengthen families and societies by empowering women to take greater control over their own destinies, cannot be fully achieved unless all governments—here and around the world—accept their responsibility to protect and promote internationally recognized human rights.

The international community has long acknowledged and recently affirmed at Vienna—that both women and men are entitled to a range of protections and personal freedoms, from the right of personal security to the right to determine freely the number and spacing of the children they bear.

No one should be forced to remain silent for fear of religious or political persecution, arrest, abuse or torture.

VIOLATIONS OF WOMEN'S HUMAN RIGHTS

Tragically, women are most often the ones whose human rights are violated.

Even in the late 20th century, the rape of women continues to be used as an instrument of armed conflict. Women and children make up a large majority of the world's refugees. When women are excluded from the political process, they become even more vulnerable to abuse.

I believe that, on the eve of a new millennium, it is time to break our silence. It is time for us to say here in Beijing, and the world to hear, that it is no longer acceptable to discuss women's rights as separate from human rights.

These abuses have continued because, for too long, the history of women has been a history of silence. Even today, there are those who are trying to silence our words.

The voices of this conference and of the women at Huairou must be heard loud and clear:

It is a violation of human rights when babies are denied food, or drowned, or suffocated, or their spines broken, simply because they are born girls.

It is a violation of human rights when women and girls are sold into the slavery of prostitution.

It is a violation of human rights when women are doused with gasoline, set on fire and burned to death because their marriage dowries are deemed too small.

It is a violation of human rights when individual women are raped in their own communities and when thousands of women are subjected to rape as a tactic or prize of war.

It is a violation of human rights when a leading cause of death worldwide among women ages 14 to 44 is the violence they are subjected to in their own homes.

It is a violation of human rights when young girls are brutalized by the painful and degrading practice of genital mutilation.

It is a violation of human rights when women are denied the right to plan their own families, and that includes being forced to have abortions or being sterilized against their will.

WOMEN'S RIGHTS ARE HUMAN RIGHTS

If there is one message that echoes forth from this conference, it is that human rights are women's rights and women's rights are human rights. Let us not forget that among those rights are the right to speak freely—and the right to be heard.

Women must enjoy the right to participate fully in the social and political lives of their countries if we want freedom and democracy to thrive and endure.

It is indefensible that many women in nongovernmental organizations who wished to participate in this conference have not been able to attend—or have been prohibited from fully taking part.

Let me be clear. Freedom means the right of people to assemble, organize, and debate openly. It means respecting the views of those who may disagree with the views of their governments. It means not taking citizens away from their loved ones and jailing them, mistreating them, or denying them their freedom or dignity because of the peaceful expression of their ideas and opinions.

A Call to Action

In my country, we recently celebrated the 75th anniversary of women's suffrage. It took 150 years after the signing of our Declaration of Independence for women to win the right to vote.

It took 72 years of organized struggle on the part of many courageous women and men. It was one of America's most divisive philosophical wars. But it was also a bloodless war. Suffrage was achieved without a shot being fired. . . .

We have seen peace prevail in most places for a half century. We have avoided another world war.

But we have not solved older, deeply-rooted problems that continue to diminish the potential of half the world's population.

Now it is time to act on behalf of women everywhere.

If we take bold steps to better the lives of women, we will be taking bold steps to better the lives of children and families too.

Families rely on mothers and wives for emotional support and care; families rely on women for labor in the home, and increasingly, families rely on women for income needed to raise healthy children and care for other relatives.

As long as discrimination and inequities remain so commonplace around the world—as long as girls and women are valued less, fed less, fed last, overworked, underpaid, not schooled, and subjected to violence in and out of their homes—the potential of the human family to create a peaceful, prosperous world will not be realized. . . .

We can create a world in which every woman is treated with respect and dignity, every boy and girl is loved and cared for equally, and every family has the hope of a strong and stable future.

Thank you very much.

God's blessings on you, your work, and all who will benefit from it.

"Far from representing the views of
the world's women, [the women's
rights agenda] represents the views
of a narrow sect of Western women."

THE WOMEN'S RIGHTS AGENDA
IGNORES THIRD WORLD CONCERNS

Anne Applebaum

Many people have argued that the human rights community has
neglected the matter of women's rights. In September 1995, the
United Nations Fourth World Conference on Women provided a
forum for those concerned with human rights for women. Anne
Applebaum contends, in the following viewpoint, that an overly
narrow women's rights agenda dominated this conference. According to Applebaum, this agenda revealed a Western feminist
bias in its focus on reproductive rights and gender studies and
neglected several issues of concern to third world women such
as poverty, illiteracy, and the family. A principled human rights
agenda should pay more than token attention to the concerns of
third world women, Applebaum maintains. Applebaum is the
deputy editor of the *Spectator*, a weekly British periodical.

As you read, consider the following questions:

1. In Applebaum's opinion, what was the fundamental
   assumption of the World Conference on Women?
2. According to Wanjiru Cithongo as quoted by Applebaum,
   why are development agencies ineffectual?
3. For what reason does the author object to the use of the
   word "gender" in the conference's "Platform for Action"?

It was late afternoon and rain was falling, making a soft drumming noise on the tent where Betty Friedan, draped in a flowing, leopard-print dress, had just been speaking about the need to "transcend polarization and create a new form of women's community." Now she was sitting silent while a Yakut woman, dressed in a stiff beige suit and a stiff white blouse, read a speech in stiffly translated French. In Yakutia, the woman explained, "mothers must be the basis of a renaissance of ethnic nationhood."

Betty Friedan raised her eyebrows.

But in Yakutia, the woman continued, stumbling over her words, "women work but they are also mothers and domestic workers," which is not an easy combination in northern Siberia.

Betty Friedan glanced at her watch.

No doubt the grandmother of American feminism—after her book The Feminine Mystique was published in 1963, millions of bored American housewives dropped their brooms, abandoned their dustpans, left their well-appointed suburban homes, and went back to work—had a touch of jet-lag. Or perhaps some forms of cross-cultural interaction are more exciting than others.

AN EXCHANGE OF IDEAS?

If anyone sensed any irony in the situation—here was a Yakut woman complaining of the difficulties of combining work and home-making, and here was Betty Friedan, who once complained of the boredom of not combining work and home-making—no one pointed it out. But then, irony was not really the reigning attitude in Huairou, the Chinese village transformed in 1995 by the addition of tents, concrete hostels, and 20,000 women from every country in the world into a veritable cornucopia of workshops, panel discussions, demonstrations, and debates.

Huairou was, of course, the site of the Non-Governmental Organizations' Forum on Women, the unofficial part of the United Nations Fourth World Conference on Women. Betty Friedan, the woman from Yakutia, and 20,000 other women were in Huairou to lobby the government officials who ultimately signed the "Platform for Action"—of which more later.

But they were also in Huairou to exchange ideas—or, as some of the many Americans would have said, simply to relate. This was less simple than it may sound. Often the women seemed divided quite fundamentally. Just a few tents down from Betty Friedan, for example, a group of somewhat confused Japanese women were explaining the work of their charity, which delivers meals to the elderly. There was a photograph of a typical meal, and there were pictures of the elderly who eat the meals, but the women seemed unsure of why they were in Huairou: "We are looking forward anxiously to understanding what other women have to say here," one told me. "We are leaving tomorrow," said another. A hundred yards further on, a group of much less confused Japanese feminists—black dresses, black sunglasses, short hair—were demonstrating against nuclear testing: "Ban All Bombs" read their banner.

A CLEAR DIVIDE

Much more fundamental, however, was the clear divide between women from the developing world and women from industrial countries. Most of the Third World women were interested in very basic issues: the horrors of female circumcision, legal systems which prevent women from owning property, hunger and illiteracy. Some of them had no right to be in China at all. In the "official" Tibetan tent, Tibetan women were handing out leaflets claiming that "various assertions" about Tibetan women are "totally groundless." Later, Tibetan women who have been expelled from their country staged protests reminding the world that Tibetan women who maintain their loyalty to the Dalai Lama risk beatings, jail, and death.

The Western agenda was somewhat different: it ranged from lesbian rights to the need for women's studies at universities to "Gender Stereotyping and Sexism in Advertising" (a workshop sponsored by the Montreal Council of Women). French women were discussing feminist theory; American women were talking about black women's literature. If that sounds like evidence of Western women's success—after all, we won the right to own property and vote long ago—that isn't the way most at Huairou would have seen it. That Western women are oppressed, and that they share their oppression with their sisters in the rest of the world, was a fundamental assumption of the conference.

It certainly did make for some odd juxtapositions, and occasionally a degree of discomfort. In the women's bookshop, the Tanzanian Media Women's Association was selling brightly printed African scarves, while the American Association for the Advancement of Science was selling textbooks (In Touch with Electricity) and answering questions about how to teach science to girls. At a workshop entitled "Politics of Difference: Single Women," a few Indians turned up expecting to talk about prostitution and the unbearable pressures brought to bear on women who want to leave unhappy arranged marriages, while a few

53

Americans turned up expecting to talk about the difficulties of living alone in Philadelphia ("People, like, think you're lesbian").

CONFLICTING VIEWS ON RIGHTS

Most of all, though, the differences underlined the fundamental absurdity of the idea that a UN conference is an appropriate place to resolve the problems of all women everywhere. "Our issues are much more basic: we need education, we need a health system that works," Wanjiru Cithongo, an articulate Kenyan woman, told me. She also felt offended that the promotion of birth control, as well as abortion, had now become the primary (sometimes the only) concern of development agencies, thanks mostly to American pressure: "Aid agencies are only talking about reproductive health, not women's total health. I can have contraceptives for free at the Planned Parenthood clinic, but if I want penicillin—which might save a child's life—no one from the outside world will pay for that."

Emmie Chanika, an even more forceful Malawian with braided hair, full tribal kit, and a better command of English than most Englishwomen, said the whole conference seemed concerned with issues that are alien to her. "Women here say they are fighting for their rights," she said, "but we differ in what we mean about rights." In Malawi, she explained, witch doctors had taken to telling men that sleeping with a girl child would make them rich: "We would like girl children to have a right not to be raped over and over again: this is a real problem. But the Western women here seem interested only in other kinds of rights"—like the right to abortion or the right to divorce or the right to live alone. (The notion of lesbian rights merely mystified her: "Let me think—do we have a word for lesbian in Malawi?")

AN AMERICAN FEMINIST BIAS

After a few days of listening to this sort of talk, it was also impossible not to feel that something was very wrong with the way that the obsessions of American feminism dominated the "official" debate in Peking. Leafing through the 149-page Platform for Action, for example, it was impossible not to note that the word "sex" almost never appears; it has been replaced by the word "gender." Although "gender" is never defined in the document, Virginia Ofusu-Amaah, head of the Gender, Population, and Development Branch (formerly the Sex, Population, and Development Branch) in the UN's Fund for Population Activities recently offered some clues, explaining that "gender refers to socially constructed roles, and gender roles change. Sex does not change." Using the expression "gender" rather than sex, in other words, implies that "women" is in fact an infinitely malleable social construct, of which biology is not necessarily the most important element.

The Needs of Third World Women

The often repeated phrase, "It takes a village to raise a child" is supposedly an African proverb. However, an African medical doctor, Margaret Ogola, said her disillusionment for hope at the U.N. Conference on Women was finished when the American delegation laughed at the fact that children need a family. She said, "Apparently the US considers the family as nothing anymore. Safer abortion is all the conference talks about, what about safe motherhood? Is it OK to die of malaria more than abortion?" She told about losing a child because of a lack of cheap medicine while there were walls of contraceptives in the next room. She called contraceptives nonsense in the face of AIDS and advocated families as preventative strength.

Cathie Adams, *Dallas/Fort Worth Heritage*, November 1995.

The words "mother" and "motherhood" rarely appeared either, presumably because those would be unacceptable, old-fashioned gender roles, clearly derived from female biology. Instead, the document bemoans the fact that the "unequal division of labor and responsibilities within households based on unequal power relations also limits women's potential . . . for participation in decision-making in wider public forums." Translating into English, I take that to mean that having children makes it hard for women to participate in public life as fully as men, and that something must be done about it.

Of course, it is hard to object to the idea that women should have access to the worlds of work and politics, particularly in societies (like ours) with high divorce rates, where most women must either have careers or risk future impoverishment. Women who don't want children, or who are wealthy enough to have nannies or lucky enough to have extended families, must be allowed the legal right to work if they need to or want to, and the legal right to own property: in the Western world, those are now accepted rights, and the many Third World women have come here to fight for those rights as well.

Ignoring the Views of the World's Women

But there is nevertheless something shocking, and unique to Western feminism, about this notion that biology can be discarded just as easily as bras can be burned, or that having children is nothing but a burden to working women, or that women's reproductive role can be neutralized through UN-recommended "government programs" and the distribution of documents like the Platform for Action. No wonder that so many Third World governments, and so many Third World women at the conference, objected to it: far from representing the views of the world's women, this document represents the views of a narrow sect of Western women, who believe that the only acceptable form of "progress" is the shedding of biology and the abandonment of the traditional family.

Only every once in a while did someone remind those in Huairou that not all such progress is good for women. As an Iranian woman explained during one workshop, "the West thinks it is progressive because it has no polygamy, as the Muslim world has. But if a man wants another woman in the West, he takes a mistress, and the wife just has to put up with it. Or he takes a second wife, and the first wife has to leave. Why is that more progressive?" At least, she pointed out, first wives maintain some rights and some status within Muslim families.

But hers was a lone voice. Of the 20,000 women in Huairou, I would guess that about half were American, and of those, I would guess that nearly all think of themselves as liberated, and therefore superior to the "unliberated" women of Africa and Asia. I would also guess that nearly all of these unliberated women—many of whom are involved in genuinely good projects (teaching girls to read, fighting against domestic violence)—maintain a degree of skepticism about the women of the West, who have abandoned some of the things which they believe to be essential.

PERIODICAL BIBLIOGRAPHY

The following articles have been selected to supplement the diverse views presented in this chapter. Addresses are provided for periodicals not indexed in the *Readers' Guide to Periodical Literature*, the *Alternative Press Index*, the *Social Sciences Index*, or the *Index to Legal Periodicals and Books*.

Philip Alston — "The Struggle for Human Rights," *Unesco Courier*, October 1995.

David Bacon — "For an Immigration Policy Based on Human Rights," *Social Justice*, Fall 1996.

Deborah L. Billings — "Sexual and Reproductive Rights: Woman-Centered, Activist Agendas," *Against the Current*, July/August 1997.

J. Kenneth Blackwell — "The Human Rights Agenda," *Vital Speeches of the Day*, November 15, 1994.

Thomas Carothers — "Democracy and Human Rights: Policy Allies or Rivals?" *Washington Quarterly*, Summer 1994.

Barbara Crossette — "Snubbing Human Rights," *New York Times*, April 28, 1996.

Paige Comstock Cunningham — "United Nations Agenda for Women Falls Short," *Christianity Today*, October 23, 1995.

Edward S. Herman — "Immiseration and Human Rights," *Z Magazine*, April 1995.

Stephen A. James — "Reconciling International Human Rights and Cultural Relativism: The Case of Female Circumcision," *Bioethics*, 1994. Available from 108 Cowley Rd., Oxford OX4 1JF, England.

Bilahari Kausikan — "Asian Versus 'Universal' Human Rights," *Responsive Community*, Summer 1997. Available from 2020 Pennsylvania Ave. NW, Suite 282, Washington, DC 20052.

Andrew J. Nathan — "China: Getting Human Rights Right," *Washington Quarterly*, Spring 1997.

Aaron Sachs — "Upholding Human Rights and Environmental Justice," *Humanist*, March/April 1996.

Amartya Sen — "Human Rights and Asian Values," *New Republic*, July 14 and 21, 1997.

Charles Taylor — "A World Consensus on Human Rights?" *Dissent*, Summer 1996.

CHAPTER 2

WHAT IS THE STATE OF HUMAN RIGHTS?

CHAPTER PREFACE

Many human rights organizations continue to focus their concerns on the plight of the world's refugees—people fleeing their home countries because they cannot depend on their governments to protect them from persecution, torture, and other human rights abuses. More than fifteen million refugees worldwide are currently seeking protection from human rights violations—nearly double the amount of refugees fleeing persecution in the late 1980s. This growth in the refugee population is largely the result of civil wars and other conflicts that broke out in many parts of the world during the 1990s.

The human rights organization Amnesty International (AI) contends that today's refugees face increasing difficulties due to "a marked deterioration in the level of international protection for refugees." AI points out that many of the world's governments are closing their countries' borders and denying refugees political asylum by introducing strict immigration measures and visa requirements. Furthermore, AI argues, several states are actively engaging in *refoulement*—the forcible repatriation of refugees to their home countries where they face death or persecution. Even though Article 33 of the UN Refugee Convention, as well as customary international law, prohibits *refoulement*, "many states violate this [rule] and return refugees to countries where they are at grave risk," AI maintains.

Advocates of immigration control contend, however, that nations should not be expected to take in unlimited numbers of refugees. They argue that in the United States, for example, the immigration of 1.1 million people a year—one-quarter of whom are political refugees—threatens the stability and manageability of an already overpopulated America. Furthermore, some experts on U.S. immigration maintain, the categories of political asylum have recently been expanded to include people with AIDS, women from male-dominated societies, and religious minorities. Critics claim that many asylees now come to the United States not to escape persecution but to gain access to American health care or to find a new home in a more open society. These critics contend that political asylum must be reevaluated so that the world's migrants do not overtax the resources of the United States.

Political asylum is just one of the topics debated in the following chapter in which commentators examine the contemporary state of human rights.

| "While the state of human rights protection in the United States has advanced significantly over the years, many challenges and problems remain."

THE UNITED STATES FACES HUMAN RIGHTS CHALLENGES

John Shattuck

John Shattuck is the assistant secretary for the Bureau of Democracy, Human Rights, and Labor, an office in the U.S. Department of State. In the following viewpoint, he argues that the United States continues to face many difficulties in the area of human rights. He concedes that progress in human rights—such as the legal protection of political freedom, civil liberties, and self-determination—has resulted because of guarantees provided by the Constitution. However, Shattuck contends, present-day injustices, such as gender discrimination and police brutality, indicate that serious human rights challenges remain. This viewpoint is excerpted from an introduction to a 1994 U.S. State Department report to the UN Human Rights Committee.

As you read, consider the following questions:

1. What are some forerunners to contemporary human rights law, according to the author?
2. According to Shattuck, what two categories of human rights have been defined by the international community?
3. Which human rights issues has the United States legal system largely addressed, in the author's opinion?

Reprinted from John Shattuck, "Civil and Political Rights in the United States," *U.S. Department of State Dispatch*, September 19, 1994.

This is the first report submitted by the United States in accordance with its obligations under an international human rights treaty. Written to UN specifications and prepared through the collaborative efforts of the U.S. Departments of State, Justice, and other executive branch departments and agencies with input from non-governmental organizations and concerned individuals, it represents a government-wide commitment to creative interaction with the emerging global framework of international human rights law. It is meant to offer to the international community a sweeping picture of human rights observance in the United States and the legal and political system within which those rights have evolved and are protected.

The International Covenant on Civil and Political Rights was concluded in 1966, entered into force 10 years later, in 1976, and was ratified by the United States in 1992. . . . A total of 127 countries have, to date, become party to the treaty. Together with the Universal Declaration of Human Rights and the International Covenant on Economic, Social, and Cultural Rights, it represents the most complete and authoritative articulation of international human rights law that has emerged in the years following World War II.

THE HISTORY OF HUMAN RIGHTS LAW

The antecedents of contemporary human rights law stretch far back into history to natural law traditions, the ethical teachings of the world's great religions—both East and West—Greco-Roman law, and the pioneering philosophical works of Hugo Grotius and John Locke. The concept of universal rights developed by 18th-century political theorists nourished international law as it also set the stage for American constitutionalism. Indeed, international human rights law and the constitutional law of the United States are, at bottom, profoundly related—both seek to limit the authority of states to interfere with the inalienable rights of all individuals, without discrimination.

The first major articulations of international human rights law took place after World War I around the creation of the ill-fated League of Nations, its system for the protection of minorities, and the more successful International Labor Organization.

It was, however, the horrific experiences of mid-century totalitarianism and World War II that spurred the victorious Allied Powers to try to inscribe into international law the larger goals that had emerged during the war, such as President Roosevelt's Four Freedoms. The Nuremberg trials—in which the vanquished Nazi leaders were publicly tried, convicted, and sentenced according to the principles of international law—represented an attempt to fashion a new international order which would work to protect human dignity and, in some measure, redeem the terrible sufferings of the victims of totalitarianism.

THE BIRTH OF THE UNITED NATIONS

The capstone of these efforts was the creation of the United Nations and the adoption of its Charter, the promulgation of the Universal Declaration of Human Rights, and the launching of the efforts that resulted in the two major covenants on international human rights.

While the League had focused on the rights of minority groups to self-determination, the UN Charter was all-embracing, making it the legal as well as the political responsibility of all member states to protect and promote the human rights and fundamental freedoms of their people.

The Universal Declaration of Human Rights, adopted unanimously by the UN General Assembly in 1948, represented an authoritative articulation of the rights that member states are generally obliged to protect and promote under the UN Charter. The declaration synthesized the two categories of human rights that have emerged in international legal discourse—civil and political rights on the one hand and economic, social, and cultural rights on the other. It has remained to the international community to sift out these distinct though related elements in order to create workable instruments of international law.

A UNIVERSAL BIRTHRIGHT

Human rights have come to be recognized as the universal birthright of every man, woman, and child on this planet. This faith in inalienable human dignity rests at the core of the international law of human rights; it has many different sources and has been articulated over time in different ways. Indeed, its commanding power rests in no small measure on the varied nature of its sources; it is not anchored in any one philosophical, religious, or ideological foundation. The Universal Declaration achieved inclusiveness precisely because it did not lodge these timeless principles in any specific and thus, inevitably, debatable and partial political program.

The Covenant on Civil and Political Rights contributes to the promotion of international human rights by codifying many of the principles we, in the United States, hold dear—political freedom; self-determination; freedom of speech, opinion, expression, association, and religion; and protection of the family against governmental intrusion. The unfortunate fact that these principles are disregarded in many countries in no way diminishes their commanding authority.

The United States as a nation was founded on the principle of inalienable individual rights. The history of this country is in many ways the story of an ongoing struggle to fulfill the promise of that conception of rights, a struggle to overcome old and new injustices in our own democracy that continues today. As part of that struggle, the United States is also firmly committed to promoting respect for human rights and fundamental freedoms around the globe. U.S. law provides extensive protection against human rights abuses by government authorities.

POLICE BRUTALITY IN THE UNITED STATES

Police brutality remained one of the most controversial and pervasive human rights problems in the United States in 1996. Police officers in a number of cities were accused of serious human rights violations, including unjustified shootings and severe beatings, with many victims asserting that these abuses were racially motivated. And even while Congress approved funding to hire thousands of new police officers in cities around the country, there was no concomitant effort to improve flawed civilian review boards, police internal investigation procedures, or the low rate of prosecution for criminal civil rights violations. According to the most recent Justice Department national data available, of 8,575 complaints reviewed under the federal civil rights statutes in 1994, only seventy-six cases were filed for prosecution—less than 1 percent.

Human Rights Watch World Report, 1996.

Under the U.S. Constitution, government authority is distributed and diffused through the separation of powers between the three branches of government. From the beginning of this nation's history, the United States Supreme Court has exercised the power of judicial review to check unconstitutional action by the executive and legislative branches. Freedoms of speech and religion are protected by law, police power is subject to significant constitutional limitations, and America's political leadership at all levels is held accountable to its citizens.

Our Constitution laid out a blueprint for the interpretation and realization of the idea of civil and political rights and freedoms, but it has taken the labors of generations of citizens from all parts of our society to build the institutions which carry the promise of these rights and freedoms. This process has unfolded over more than two centuries, through many chapters of history—some noble and others dark—and the task continues to this day.

HUMAN RIGHTS VIOLATIONS IN AMERICA

Over the course of its history, America has experienced egregious human rights violations in this ongoing American struggle for justice, such as the enslavement and disenfranchisement of African Americans and the virtual destruction of many Native American civilizations.

The profound injustices visited on African Americans were only partially erased after the Civil War (1861–65), and then, a century later, by the civil rights movement of the 1950s and 1960s—a movement that combined heroic leadership with grassroots organizing and dogged legal marches through courthouses and legislatures, a movement that helped shape the interpretation and implementation of constitutional law to ensure that human rights could be respected in practice.

Those efforts to undo the bitter legacy of slavery continue today. The lessons learned from our nation's unfinished battle with racial discrimination can be shared with other members of the international community. Simply put, our national experience demonstrates that legal guarantees of human rights are a prerequisite to social progress, not the other way around.

Native Americans have suffered a fate similar to that of many indigenous civilizations—destruction and displacement of their cultures and societies. The lessons of those injustices and the responsibilities with which the people of the United States are charged as a result are also central legacies of American history.

DISCRIMINATION AND INJUSTICE

The members of other minority groups have suffered injustices in the United States. The United States is largely a nation of immigrants. We continue to draw wave after wave of men and women from around the world seeking a better life, with annual immigration now surpassing 900,000. However, immigrants to our shores—like immigrants everywhere—have often met with discrimination and resistance that have deepened the personal dislocations of migration. The openness of our society has permitted, with time, mobility and release from poverty and marginalization. In the process, immigrant groups themselves have deeply enriched our national identity, as the 19th century's notion of a "melting pot" of assimilation has gradually given way to a broader vision of pluralism.

The ongoing struggle for full realization of the rights of women is a central feature of the human rights process in America. Women did not have the vote in the United States until 1920, a century and a half after the founding of the republic. With growing strength, women have moved to claim their equal place in the political, economic, and social life of the country. Efforts are underway in all sectors of American life to broaden women's opportunities and end remaining discrimination.

There are many other human rights challenges in our nation's historical and contemporary experience. As we have continued to find new challenges, we have worked with varying degrees of success to strengthen the capacity of our institutions to address them.

Addressing Human Rights Issues

As an open democracy, the United States tends to address its most difficult and divisive human rights issues in public and in the courts. The result is a number of long-standing human rights issues with a large body of case law, as well as many newer issues on which legal ground is being broken. Among the former are such areas as freedom of religion, immigrants and refugees, race discrimination, and freedom of expression. More recent areas of concern include gender discrimination, the death penalty, abortion, police brutality, and language rights.

As a matter of domestic law, treaties as well as statutes must conform to the requirements of the Constitution. No treaty provision will be given effect as U.S. law if it conflicts with the Constitution. In the case of the Covenant on Civil and Political Rights, the U.S. Constitution offers greater protection of free speech than does the Covenant. On those and some other provisions of the Covenant, the United States has recorded its understanding of a particular provision or made a declaration of how it intends to apply that provision or undertaking.

It is of little use to proclaim principles of human rights protection at the international level unless they can be meaningfully realized and enforced domestically. In the words of the renowned human rights and constitutional scholar Louis Henkin, "The international law of human rights parallels and supplements national law . . . but it does not replace, and indeed depends on, national institutions." Thus, it is up to the various organs of federal, state, and local government here in the United States to bring those international commitments to fruition.

As observers have noted ever since the great French thinker and statesman Alexis de Tocqueville penned his classic *Democracy in*

America in the 1830s, the United States possesses a strikingly robust legal and judicial system, and it is in and through that system that legal protection for human rights has taken shape. . . .

The broad conception of rights that has evolved in the course of U.S. history has come to serve as the basis for much of international human rights law and, ironically but fittingly, to set the standard by which the United States is judged by other members of the international community.

A WORK IN PROGRESS

While the state of human rights protection in the United States has advanced significantly over the years, many challenges and problems remain. The elaborate structure of human rights law emerged in the course of a long and painful struggle in the United States in a sweeping historical narrative displaying cruelty and injustice alongside vision and courage. It has been a distinguishing characteristic of our political and legal system to weave the constant possibility of change into the fabric of constitutional democracy. . . .

Here, as elsewhere, the realization of universal human rights is a work in progress. While the U.S. system has done much over time to advance and champion human rights, much remains to be done. The U.S. Government welcomes the spirited dialogue and debate on the advancement of human rights in the United States and throughout the global community that is taking shape on the horizon of the 21st century.

"It [is not] easy to understand how we have come to tolerate public officials who see nothing wrong with attacking their own country in an international forum."

THE UNITED STATES DESERVES NO CRITICISM ON HUMAN RIGHTS

Midge Decter

The United States is one of the freest nations in the world and therefore deserves no negative evaluation of its record on human rights, contends Midge Decter in the following viewpoint. She maintains that government officials' denouncements of the status of human rights in the United States are unwarranted—particularly in light of the widescale poverty, torture, and murder that occurs in many other nations. Decter is a distinguished fellow at the Institute on Religion and Public Life, a conservative public policy organization in New York City.

As you read, consider the following questions:

1. What issues must governments provide information about in their human rights reports to the United Nations, according to Decter?
2. In the author's opinion, what is the problem with the implication that the death penalty is a violation of human rights?
3. What is spiritual greed, in Decter's opinion?

As the diplomatic arm of the world's greatest power, the U.S. Department of State has many, and widely varied, responsibilities. In 1992, the Bush administration added one more: by agreeing, after the country had held out for sixteen years, to sign the United Nations International Covenant on Civil and Political Rights, it placed upon the State Department the responsibility for the preparation of an annual report on the condition of human rights in the U.S.

On September 28, 1994, the first such report, a closely printed document of 213 pages, was submitted to the UN Human Rights Committee. As might be expected, this report was undertaken under the supervision of the State Department office formerly known as Human Rights and Humanitarian Affairs and now, for some reason, called Democracy, Human Rights, and Labor. The major obligation of this office in the past was to submit to the Congress annual reports on human rights around the world, country by country. Now it is obligated to report to the world organization on its own country as well.

THE REPORT TO THE UNITED NATIONS

The format for reporting to the UN is carefully prescribed. It demands coverage of the country's treatment of a whole range of rights and protections, from something as straightforward and simple as the right to a fair trial or the right to freedom of movement, to issues as multifaceted and controversial as the rights of women, the protection of the family, and the rights of minorities in the areas of culture, religion, and language.

In accordance with this prescription, the U.S. report, after a general introduction to the country's demography, economy, and political institutions, consists mainly of a compendium of statutes, federal and state, as well as an account of case law dealing with what the UN defines as human-rights issues. It has clearly been an enormous, and enormously painstaking, job to produce this document; many man-hours in the State and Justice departments, along with other agencies, must have gone into it.

It would seem, however, that while Assistant Secretary of State for Democracy, Human Rights, and Labor John Shattuck supervised the preparation of this report, in the end he himself was disappointed with the result. Or possibly he found the prescribed format too limiting to encompass his own view of the subject. In any event, in early September 1994, he deemed it advisable to tack on to the body of the report a special introduction intended to add some further clarification about the state of human rights in the United States.

Mr. Shattuck begins his introduction with a brief but heartfelt historical survey of human-rights law in general, whose antecedents, he tells us, stretch back "to natural-law traditions, the ethical teachings of the world's great religions—both East and West—Greco-Roman law, and the pioneering philosophical work of Hugo Grotius and John Locke." The concept of universal rights, developed in the 18th century, both "nourished international law" and "set the stage for American constitutionalism." Then, the creation of the League of Nations following World War I provided a major articulation of international human-rights law. And finally after World War II the Allied powers undertook to inscribe Franklin D. Roosevelt's Four Freedoms into international law, an effort whose capstone was the establishment of the UN and the adoption of its Charter, followed by its two major covenants of international human rights. "Human rights," says Mr. Shattuck, "have come to be recognized as the universal birthright of every man, woman, and child on this planet."

The commanding power of this faith in inalienable human dignity, he continues, resides in the fact that it is not anchored in any particular philosophical, religious, or ideological foundation. The UN's Universal Declaration of Human Rights, adopted by the General Assembly in 1948, "achieved inclusiveness precisely because it did not lodge these timeless principles in any specific, and thus inevitably debatable and partial, political program."

THE UNITED STATES AND HUMAN RIGHTS

Having thus provided a sketchy general background, the introduction gets down to the case at hand—the United States. While the American Constitution laid out a blueprint for the realization of the idea of civil and political rights, Mr. Shattuck is eager for us to understand that building the institutions to embody this blueprint has been a long, slow process involving many generations of citizens, "and the task continues to this day." The main body of the report demonstrates that, in Shattuck's own words, U.S. law "provides extensive protection against human-rights abuses by government authorities."

Indeed, the broad conception of rights that has evolved in the course of American history has come to serve as the basis for much of international human-rights law, "and, ironically but fittingly, to set the standard by which the United States is judged by other members of the international community." We must not, then, forget that "Over the course of its history, America has experienced egregious human-rights violations. . . ."

Primary among these violations, Mr. Shattuck reminds us, have been the "enslavement and disenfranchisement of African Americans and the virtual destruction of many Native American civilizations." This history, too, he traces briefly, pointing out how the injustices to blacks persisted after their emancipation and how the heroic and dogged work of the civil-rights movement of the 1950's and 1960's helped to shape both the interpretation and the implementation of constitutional law. "Those efforts to undo the bitter legacy of slavery," he concludes, "continue today."

As for Native Americans, they

> have suffered a fate similar to that of many indigenous civilizations: destruction and displacement of their cultures and societies. The lessons of those injustices . . . are also central legacies of American history.

Nor, in Mr. Shattuck's view, are African and Native Americans the only minority groups to have suffered injustice in the United States. America is largely a nation of immigrants, he informs us; annual immigration to the U.S. even today surpasses 900,000; and both socially and economically, these new ethnic minorities often meet with discrimination. And we must also bear in mind the "ongoing struggle for full realization of the rights of women . . . a central feature of the human-rights process in America."

Summing up these dark aspects of the American experience, Mr. Shattuck explains that since the U.S. tends to address its most difficult and divisive human-rights issues through the courts, there are now many areas in which new legal ground is being broken, such as "gender discrimination, the death penalty, abortion, police brutality, and language rights."

NEW LEGAL GROUND?

An interesting phenomenon, Mr. Shattuck's little essay. But first, a textual problem: what does he mean when he writes that new legal ground is being broken in such areas as the death penalty, abortion, and language rights?

As to the death penalty, is he implying that it is a violation of human rights and should therefore be abolished? If so, what does this say about the President at whose pleasure he serves, and who is so fervent a supporter of capital punishment that as governor of Arkansas he refused against much pressure to stop the execution of a retarded man? Is Bill Clinton to be condemned for a crime against human rights? And how can the

70

President sign a document taking such a position on capital punishment?

As for abortion, does Mr. Shattuck regard it as a human right? If so, what new legal ground remains to be broken? To make it available on demand, and at government expense, under any and all circumstances?

Most puzzling of all is Mr. Shattuck's mention of "language rights." With bilingual education already rampant in the U.S., what new ground does Mr. Shattuck want broken here? To ensure that every ethnic group in America is educated, and also helped by government to carry on a good deal of life's business, in the language of its country of origin?

EDUCATION FOR WHOM?

Another practical question one feels impelled to ask Mr. Shattuck about his introduction is to whom it is addressed. At one point he indicates that he wishes the report, presumably including his introduction, to be given wide distribution in order to "foster human-rights education in the United States." Forgetting about whether it is quite proper for the State Department to undertake a domestic educational campaign of this kind, why is it necessary? Is there anyone left in America who does not know that until 30 years ago the blacks had a most unhappy history in this country? Is there anyone, at least anyone who goes to the movies now and then, who does not know full well about how the white man wiped out the Indian's way of life? (On the other hand, in the interest of Mr. Shattuck's own "human-rights education," it might not be amiss for him to read, or maybe reread, the works of the great American historian Francis Parkman on how human rights fared among many of the Indian tribes themselves, particularly with respect to the treatment of captives, who were tortured as a matter of course and always with fiendish glee.)

Perhaps, then, Mr. Shattuck's introduction is intended after all for the UN Human Rights Committee, at virtually every meeting of which down through the years American delegates have had to endure moral instruction from the representatives of tyrannical, if not downright criminal, governments. Perhaps he has added this introduction to the report in order, to borrow his own words, "to set the standard by which the United States is judged by other members of the international community"— members like Iraq, Iran, Saudi Arabia, Pakistan, China, not to mention several countries in sub-Saharan Africa. Perhaps, as the man in charge of the bureau called Democracy, Human Rights, and Labor, Mr. Shattuck thought it might be democratic, humane, and supportive of all those bureaucratic laborers in the international vineyard to help them, in current parlance, feel good about themselves.

DEMEANING AMERICA

But of course Mr. Shattuck's introduction really has nothing to do with educating the American public or even with consoling his country's detractors. It springs from the same moral and intellectual source as the declaration, in song and story and schoolbook, during the celebration in 1992 of the 500th anniversary of Columbus's voyage of discovery, that the arrival of Europeans in the New World was nothing less than a major human tragedy. A more recent example of the same kind of thing was the Smithsonian Institution's effort to depict the Japanese as the victims of American aggression and cultural imperialism in World War II. (Can the poor Nazis be far behind?)

CONSPICUOUS BENEVOLENCE

For many Americans, the politics of victimization has taken the place of more traditional expressions of morality and equity. "The simple act of naming and identifying victims becomes a substitute for conscience and public discourse," writes Joseph Amato. "Identifying oneself with the 'real suffering' of a chosen class, people, group, race, sex, or historical victim is the communion call of the twentieth-century secular individual. It is his sincerity, his holiness, his martyrdom."

Political discourse and academic research alike have become dominated by what University of Chicago sociologist James Coleman calls the politics of "conspicuous benevolence," which is designed to "display, ostentatiously even, egalitarian intentions." Among his academic colleagues, Coleman gibes, postures of conspicuous benevolence have replaced "the patterns of conspicuous consumption that Thorstein Veblen attributed to the rich. . . . They display, conspicuously, the benevolent intentions of their supporters."

Charles J. Sykes, *A Nation of Victims*, 1992.

What accounts for a state of mind in which certain citizens—and even high officials—of the freest society visible to the naked human eye find it morally attractive to demean, denigrate, and even vilify that society on every possible occasion (even if, as in the case of the Smithsonian, doing so requires the telling of outright lies)?

A common answer to this question is idealism: John Shattuck and his ilk seek a never-ending process of social improvement. Another, related, answer often given is guilt: the felt need to atone for past injustices. But it hardly serves any ideal purpose to make an invidious judgment of a decent society in the face of the massive torture, murder, and manufactured starvation going on in so many other societies. And so far as guilt is concerned, the "we" who most loudly proclaim it always turn out to be talking not about their own wonderful selves but about everyone else, especially you and me.

SPIRITUAL GREED

The real answer, I believe, is greed. Not material but spiritual greed, the lust (as the feminists say in a different context) to have it all: to be freer than anyone has ever been and at the same time to go about trumpeting the ways in which one's freedom is intolerably restricted; to be privileged and yet to claim the pleasures and moral prerogatives of victimization.

It is not easy to understand how American society has come in recent years to stir so much spiritual greed in the souls of so many of those into whose hands it places great social and cultural—and even political—power. Nor is it easy to understand how we have come to tolerate public officials who see nothing wrong with attacking their own country in an international forum, and who seem to believe that there is something positively noble about acts of national self-abasement.

Must one conclude that ingratitude increases as privilege does? If that is the case—and Mr. Shattuck's essay on human rights suggests that it is—then maybe what this country needs is a little more of that process known to the sociologists as the circulation of elites.

| "Children [workers] are often
exposed to significant health hazards
and subjected to extreme physical,
verbal and even sexual abuse."

THE USE OF CHILD LABOR VIOLATES HUMAN RIGHTS

Bruce Weiner

In the following viewpoint, Bruce Weiner argues that the use of child labor constitutes an abuse of human rights. He maintains that child laborers in underdeveloped countries work for poor wages, face long workdays in unhealthy environments, receive little or no education, and are often abused. Contending that such realities violate international human rights standards, Weiner concludes that worldwide effort should be invested in eliminating the use of child labor. Weiner is the editor of *Working People*, a quarterly magazine that focuses on labor issues.

As you read, consider the following questions:

1. According to Weiner, why are accurate statistics on child labor difficult to obtain?
2. What kind of work do child laborers do, according to the author?
3. In Weiner's opinion, why is the elimination of child labor in the interest of American workers?

Reprinted from Bruce Weiner, "The Tragedy of Child Labor," *Working People*, Summer 1996, by permission.

In May 1996, Kathie Lee Gifford went on national TV to issue a tearful denial that her Wal-Mart line of clothing was produced by child labor in Honduras. In June 1996, reports surfaced that Michael Jordan's line of Nike sneakers was made by children in Indonesia working for 19 cents an hour.

Because of the ties to big names such as Kathie Lee Gifford and Michael Jordan, the child labor issue has recently won major headlines in newspapers and magazines across the country. But the problem of child labor is nothing new.

CHILDREN AS WORKERS

Early in the twentieth century, there was extensive use of child labor here in the U.S. as Americans worked through the growing pains of converting from an agricultural to an industrial economy. Although effectively eliminated from the U.S. today, the exploitation of children as workers exists as a major problem in many parts of the world. Estimates by human rights experts are that there are as many as 200 million children under the age of 14 who are working full-time. Because these children are paid little and do not receive an education, they have little chance of breaking the cycle of poverty in which they are caught.

The child labor problem is predominantly confined to underdeveloped countries. The economic reality is that children are typically paid one-half to one-third what is paid to adults doing comparable work. The children are often exposed to significant health hazards and subjected to extreme physical, verbal and even sexual abuse. While many children work to add to the family income, others are literally sold into bondage by their parents in return for money or credit.

DEFINING CHILD LABOR

In 1994, Congress directed the Department of Labor to conduct a review to identify foreign industries and their host countries that utilize child labor in the export of manufactured products to the United States. In conducting that review, the Labor Department used the definition of child labor established by the 1973 International Labor Organization Convention:

> The minimum age . . . should not be less than the age of compulsory schooling and, in any case, shall not be less than 15 years . . . countries whose economy and educational facilities are insufficiently developed [are allowed] to initially specify a minimum age of 14 years and reduce from 13 years to 12 years the minimum age for light work.

The Convention did not explicitly define "light work," other than it should not result in harming the health or development of young people and that it not interfere with their attendance at school or participation in vocational or training programs.

THE SCALE OF THE PROBLEM

The Labor Department, in completing its Congressionally mandated review, quickly discovered that the scale of the child labor problem around the world is difficult to accurately evaluate because statistics are often hard to come by and of questionable validity. Many governments, especially among developing countries, lack the facilities to obtain accurate data on child labor practices. Frequently, these governments are also reluctant to document what is not only a violation of international standards but often illegal under their own laws, reflecting a serious failure of their domestic policy.

In spite of the limits in obtaining valid data, the International Labor Office (ILO) has estimated that the total number of child workers across the globe is 100–200 million. According to the ILO, more than 95 percent of child workers live in developing countries, with Asia accounting for more than half. In Africa, an estimated one in three children work, and in Latin America, the estimate is between 15 and 20 percent.

Children work in a wide range of economic activities. The greatest number work in family-based agriculture, services (domestic servants, restaurants and street vending), prostitution and in small-scale manufacturing (e.g., carpets, garments and furniture). Export industries that most commonly employ children include garments, carpets, shoes, small-scale mining, gem-polishing and food processing.

In some cases, government policies that promote exports of low-skilled, labor intensive products, such as garments and carpets, result in an increase in the demand for and use of child labor. The Labor Department concluded that without strong international pressure and corresponding international assistance to developing countries, child labor is likely to continue unabated.

In spite of the recent publicity that Wal-Mart clothing and Nike shoe products have received, targeting the use of child labor in a particular export industry can be quite difficult. The complex arrangements between a series of middlemen between the exporter and primary producer are frequently able to disguise the use of child labor. In addition, in industries such as shoe and garment manufacturing, parts fabricated in one country are sent to a second country for assembly before being exported to the United States.

When Nike was recently accused of having Michael Jordan's line of sneakers made by 11-year-olds in Indonesia at 14 cents an hour, Nike officials pointed to the fact that the sneakers carry the label "Made in Taiwan." That label, however, only indicates that the final assembly was done in Taiwan. It does not mean, however, that no portion of the sneaker line is made in Indonesia.

WHY CHILDREN WORK

Why are children forced to work when adult unemployment is so high in these under-developed countries? There is a consensus among experts that child workers are generally less demanding, more obedient and less likely to object to their treatment or working conditions than adults. Children can also be easily taken advantage of and often are. The great majority of child workers work long hours for substandard wages under unhealthful conditions. They have few if any legal rights, can be fired without recourse and are often abused. While a few may be relatively well off compared with their peers, almost all are deprived of an adequate education.

©1997 Golliver for the *Big Bend Sentinel*: Reprinted with permission.

The reasons why children work are many and often complex. Those seeking to explain the use of child labor frequently point to traditional patterns of economic behavior and maintain that child labor is a time-honored and inevitable fact of life. They view poverty and survival as the driving forces and often maintain that a significant reduction in child labor will only occur with industrialization and rapid economic growth.

Advocates for children's rights challenge this analysis as too simplistic. They note that economic and social conditions vary from region to region and country to country. They argue that while poverty may be one very important contributing factor, other factors must also be taken into consideration. Varying by country, they also point to:

- Economic self-interest. Factory owners who overwork, underpay and otherwise take advantage of vulnerable children.
- Public indifference. Politicians, media and other public institutions who treat child labor as a non-issue.
- Public policy. Export promotion policies that support industries without regard to their impact on child labor and inadequate resources devoted to education.
- Government corruption. Government officials who not only condone but in many cases personally benefit from child labor.
- Societal prejudice. Major portions of society that consider child labor among the less privileged a part of the natural order.

In summary, children work for a variety of reasons. Some work simply to survive. Others, in the absence of free and compulsory education, lack a meaningful educational alternative. Tragically, too many children, those in bonded labor, work to repay debts incurred by their parents. Still others are kidnapped or recruited by unscrupulous agents to work away from home as a source of cheap labor. While most apologists cite poverty as the principal cause of child labor, the amount of money earned by most child workers is generally a small contribution to the family income. Although children work because they are the victims of poverty, by working instead of being educated, they tend to perpetuate the poverty cycle.

CHILD LABOR IN INDONESIA

An estimated 2.7 million children are actively working in Indonesia, according to a 1994 report by the United Nations Human Rights Commission. Although the extent of child labor in export industries is hard to measure, there is credible evidence of its use in the garment, food processing, furniture, footwear and mining industries. According to the Department of Labor report:

Children begin work at the age of nine or ten, and enter full-time wage labor after leaving primary school at the age of 12 or 13. Most children work full-time, seven hours per day, and six days a week. . . . In general, children are paid 6,000 to 9,000 Indonesian rupiahs (approximately $3.40–$5.10) per week.

Although Indonesia was one of the first countries to join the International Labor Organization's Program on the Elimination of Child Labor, according to a U.S. State Department report on Indonesian Human Rights Practices, the Indonesian government, which continues to "commit serious human rights abuses" throughout the country, has done little to try and stem the growing tide of child labor use.

It is estimated that there are over 2.5 million children working in Indonesia, in spite of an unemployment rate for adults of over 30% and a federal minimum wage of only $2.25.

IQBAL MASIH IN PAKISTAN

On April 16th, 1995, the shotgun slaying of a 12-year-old boy in a remote Pakistani village drew international headlines. The boy, Iqbal Masih, had just a year earlier been the youngest recipient of the international Reebok Human Rights Youth in Action Award. Unfortunately, Iqbal's story as a child laborer is not uncommon in today's Pakistan.

At the age of 4, Iqbal was sold into bonded labor by his father for $12. For six years he was forced to work 16 hours a day in a carpet factory. At the age of 10, Iqbal escaped from his bondage and began to speak out against the abuses of child labor in Pakistan. His efforts eventually gained international attention and the Reebok Human Rights Award. Unfortunately, the attention he drew to the problem was also, most believe, the cause of his untimely death at the hands of a still unknown assassin.

Pakistan is a poor country, with huge extremes in income distribution. Its per capita income is $450 per year, and it has a high rate of illiteracy. According to a recent U.S. State Department report, although the Pakistani government has pledged to address human rights concerns, particularly those involving women and child labor, "the overall human rights situation remains difficult."

It is estimated that more than 10 million children work in Pakistan, working 6 days a week at up to 10 hours per day. Children are used extensively in the carpet and soccer ball industries because their small hands and nimble fingers enable them to become particularly adept at weaving and stitching. Although Pakistan has put laws in effect to restrict the use of child labor, the government lacks the resources to enforce them. The lack of any federal requirement for compulsory education is also a major factor contributing to the continued use of child labor.

WHAT SHOULD BE DONE?

Advocates for children's rights are divided as to the best strategy to address the problems of child labor. Many advocate abolishing child labor immediately; they argue that in the long run, developing countries would benefit both economically and socially from a public policy of strict enforcement of both compulsory education and minimum age laws. They argue that many countries actually have the resources for greater investment in education but lack the necessary political will. They believe that strict enforcement of both compulsory education and child labor laws would be much easier to administer than a more differentiated system and would reduce opportunities for corruption.

The majority of children's rights advocates, however, believe that the immediate abolition of all child labor is unrealistic. They recommend that the first priority should be to abolish the most abusive forms of child labor, i.e., child prostitution, bonded labor and hazardous working conditions.

There is little likelihood, however, that the child labor problem will improve without a concerted international effort led by the major industrialized countries. In the U.S., efforts to bring pressure to bear on offending countries through the threatened reduction of foreign aid and restriction on imports have so far failed. The U.S., because of its position as the world's largest importer, could wield significant influence over the child labor issue. The influence of retailers and consumers' desires for cheap products, however, has left Congress reluctant to act.

American workers must decide whether they're willing to sacrifice some of those bargains to help children in foreign countries and the protection of their own jobs here at home. If child labor is eliminated, it may give a boost to economies in under-developed nations. That, in turn, would raise the overall world economy, which includes the U.S. The bottom line is that fighting child labor is not only the morally correct thing to do, but is also in the long-term self-interest of American workers.

| "In poor families it is simply understood that everyone has to work."

THE USE OF CHILD LABOR DOES NOT ALWAYS VIOLATE HUMAN RIGHTS

Shahidul Alam

The humanitarian effort to stop the use of child labor includes a congressional bill, first introduced in 1992 by Senator Tom Harkin, which would ban the importation of goods made by children. Shahidul Alam in the following viewpoint discourages such efforts. Children factory workers in third world countries contribute needed income to their households, the author points out, and these children face increased poverty or exploitative work if they are forced to leave their factory jobs. The complexity of the child labor issue must be reexamined if human rights activists truly want to improve the lives of working children, Alam contends. Alam is a photographer, writer, and activist in Dhaka, Bangladesh.

As you read, consider the following questions:

1. According to Alam, what did former children garment workers in Bangladesh do to earn income after they lost their jobs in 1994?
2. Why do factory owners like to hire children, according to the author?
3. How is the United States displaying hypocrisy in addressing the issue of child labor, in Alam's opinion?

Reprinted from Shahidul Alam, "Thank you, Mr. Harkin, Sir!" *New Internationalist*, July 1997, by permission; ©1997 by The New Internationalist.

No. No photographs. Saleha is scared. Many a time she has hidden under tables, been locked up in the toilet, or been sent to the roof in the scorching sun for two or three hours. It happens whenever foreign buyers enter the factory. She knows she is under-age, and doesn't want photographers messing things up—she needs the job. The whole industry has suddenly become sensitive. Owners want their factories open. The workers want their jobs. The special schools for former child labourers want aid money. No photographs.

Neither Saleha nor any of the other child workers I have interviewed have ever heard of Senator Tom Harkin. All they know is that pressure from the US, which buys most of Bangladesh's garments, has resulted in thousands of them losing their jobs at a stroke.

According to a press release by the garment employers in October 1994: '50,000 children lost their jobs because of the Harkin Bill'. A UNICEF worker confirms the 'jobs went overnight'.

THE EFFECTS OF THE HARKIN BILL

The controversial bill, the 'Child Labor Deterrence Act,' had first been introduced in 1992. A senior International Labour Organization (ILO) official has no doubt that the original bill was put forward 'primarily to protect US trade interests'—Tom Harkin is sponsored by a key US trade union, and cheap imports from the Third World were seen as undercutting American workers' jobs. 'When we all objected to this aspect of the Bill,' says the ILO official, 'which included a lot of resistance in the US, the Bill was amended, the trading aspect was toned down, and it was given a humanitarian look.' It was when it was reintroduced after these amendments in 1993 that the Bill had its devastating impact in Bangladesh.

The child workers themselves find it particularly hard to interpret the US approach as one of 'humanitarian concern'. When asked why the buyers have been exerting such pressure against child labour, Moyna, a ten-year-old orphan who has just lost her job, comments: 'They loathe us, don't they? We are poor and not well educated, so they simply despise us. That is why they shut the factories down.' Moyna's job had supported her and her grandmother but now they must both depend on relatives.

Other children have had no alternative but to seek new kinds of work. When UNICEF and the ILO made a series of follow-up visits they found that the children displaced from the garment factories were working at stone-crushing and street hustling—more hazardous and exploitative activities than their factory jobs.

'It is easier for the boys to get jobs again,' Moyna complains, pointing to ex-garment boys who have jobs in welding and bicycle factories. Girls usually stay at home, doing household work and looking after smaller children; many end up getting married simply to ease money problems.

RETHINKING CHILD LABOUR

In the wake of the mass expulsion of child garment workers it was plain that something had gone very wrong. UNICEF and the ILO tried to pick up the pieces. After two years of hard talking with the garment employers they came up with a Memorandum of Understanding. This guaranteed that no more children under 14 would be hired, that existing child workers would be received into special schools set up by local voluntary organizations and would receive a monthly stipend to compensate them for the loss of their wages.

Some garment owners feel that, instead of doing a deal, they should have called the US bluff and continued employing young children. 'We export 150 million shirts a year to the US,' says one. 'The K-mart $12 shirt would have cost $24. Bill Clinton would have lost his job.'

As of now 10,547 of the estimated 50,000 children have been registered, and of these 8,067 have enlisted in school. Most weren't registered initially, as few garment owners admitted having children working in their factories. Many lost their jobs before the registration process began. Unregistered children, regardless of their age or their schooling, are not admitted into the scheme.

Saleha is tall for her age. Though in her factory there are quite a few under-age children, in most factories children that look small are no longer taken. This is what Moyna and Ekram and the other children repeatedly say: 'We didn't make the size.' In a country where births are not registered there is no way of accurately determining a person's age. Children with good growth keep their jobs. Children who look smaller, perhaps because they are malnourished, do not.

SABEENA'S STORY

The reliance on size rather than age means that many children are still at work in the factories—and many have no inclination to take up a place in one of the special schools. Take Sabeena. Her factory is colourful with tinsel when I visit and many of the girls have glitter on their faces. It is the Bangla New Year and Eid all in one and they are celebrating. Sabeena proudly shows me the machine she works on. She is almost 14 and, like Saleha, big for her age. She has been working at a garment factory ever since she finished Grade Five, about 18 months ago. Until then, schooling was free. There was no way her parents could pay for her to go to school and, with her father being poorly, Sabeena needed to work to keep the family going.

What Working Children Want

1. We want recognition of our problems, our initiatives, proposals and our process of organization.

2. We are against the boycott of products made by children.

3. We want respect and security for ourselves and the work that we do.

4. We want an education system whose methodology and content are adapted to our reality.

5. We want professional training adapted to our reality and capabilities.

6. We want access to good healthcare for working children.

7. We want to be consulted on all decisions concerning us, at local, national or international level.

8. We want the root causes of our situation, primarily poverty, to be addressed and tackled.

9. We want more activity in rural areas so that children do not have to migrate to the cities.

10. We are against exploitation at work but we are for work with dignity, with hours adapted so that we have time for education and leisure.

Child Delegates, First International Conference on Working Children, November 1996.

Taking home 2,200 taka ($52) a month (with overtime) Sabeena, at 13, is now the main breadwinner in the family. She is lucky to have work, though she would rather study. She laughs when I talk of her going to school. She has mouths to feed, and to give up her job for a 300-taka-per-month stipend for going to school simply wouldn't make sense. Besides, the special schools only teach up to Grade Five. The better students, who have studied that far, find they have neither jobs nor seats in the school. So Sabeena's studies begin at around eleven at night, with a paid private tutor, usually by candlelight. At seven in the morning she has to leave for work. Seven days a week.

THE NEED FOR PAID WORK

Money is a key concern even for those children who have been received into the special schools. At the school run by the Bangladesh Rural Advancement Committee (BRAC) in Mirpur, the children gather round a worker doing the rounds. 'When do we get paid, sir?' they keep asking.

Despite the promises, not a single child that I have interviewed has received the full pay they are owed. In some cases field workers, eager to improve their admission rates, have promised considerably more than the stipulated 300 taka ($7) per month. In others, unfounded rumours have created expectations that the schools cannot meet.

Shahjahan was one of the lucky ones admitted to a BRAC school. The 300 taka per month is a small sum for him too, but he works in a tailoring shop from nine till eleven in the morning, and again from two-thirty in the afternoon till ten at night. He doesn't complain. Though the scheme does not encourage it, he feels he is getting the best of both worlds: free schooling, including a stipend, as well as paid work and a potential career.

Did they like working in garment factories? The children find this a strange question. They earned money because of it, and it gave them a certain status that non-working children did not have. They put up with the long hours. The exceptions remind me that it is children we are talking about. 'I cried when they forced me to do overtime on Thursday nights,' says Moyna. 'That was when they showed Alif Laila (Arabian Nights) on TV.'

Child workers are popular with factory owners. 'Ten- to twelve-year-olds are the best,' says Farooq, the manager of Sabeena's factory. 'They are easier to control, not interested in men, or movies, and obedient.' He forgets to mention that they are not unionized and that they agree to work for 500 taka ($12) per month when the minimum legal wage for a helper is 930 taka.

THE REALITIES OF GARMENT WORKERS' LIVES

Owners see Tom Harkin as a well-meaning soul with little clue about the realities of garment workers' lives. 'As a student, I too hailed the Bill,' says Sohel, the production manager at Captex Garments. 'I was happy that someone was fighting for children's rights. But now that I work in a factory and have to turn away these children who need jobs, I see things differently. Sometimes I take risks and, if a child is really in a bad way, I let them work, but it is dangerous.'

The notion that a garment employer might be helping children by allowing them to work may seem very strange to people in the West. But in a country where the majority of people live in villages where children work in the home and the fields as part of growing up, there are no romantic notions of childhood as an age of innocence. Though children are cared for, childhood is seen as a period for learning employable skills. Children have always helped out with family duties. When this evolves into a paid job in the city neither children nor their families see it as anything unusual. In poor families it is simply understood that everyone has to work.

The money that children earn is generally handed over to parents, who run the household as best they can. Most parents want their children to go to school. But they also feel that schooling is a luxury they cannot afford. The garment industry has increased the income of working-class families in recent years and this has also led to a change in attitudes. Many middle-class homes now complain that it is difficult to get domestic 'help' as working-class women and children choose to work in garment factories rather than as servants. This choice—made on the grounds not just of better economics, but of greater self-respect—is one many children have lost because of the Harkin Bill.

US HYPOCRISY

The US is wielding power without responsibility. A nation with a history of genocide and slavery, and a reputation for being a bully in international politics, suddenly proclaims itself a champion of people's rights, but refuses to make concessions over the rates it will pay. The dollar price-tags on the garments produced in some factories suggest a vast profit being made at the US end. The buyers claim that what they pay for the garments is determined by 'market forces'. The garment owners make the same claim with regard to the conditions of employment for their workers. Both are simply justifying their own version of exploitation—and to address child labour without addressing exploitation is to treat the symptom, not the disease.

The garment-industry experience has led to an active debate amongst development workers and child-rights activists. 'What we have done here in Bangladesh is described as fantastic,' says a senior ILO worker. 'I wonder how fantastic it really is. How much difference will these two or three years in school make to these children? In three years, the helper could have been an operator, with better pay and more savings. Even if the manufacturers keep their word and give them back their jobs at the end of their schooling, the Memorandum children will hardly be better off, while their peers will have gotten on with their careers. We have spent millions of dollars on 8,000 children. The money itself could have transformed their lives. This is an experiment by the donors, and the Bangladeshi children have to pay.'

"[The growing number of refugees] is the predictable consequence of human rights crises throughout the world."

REFUGEES FACE BARRIERS TO POLITICAL ASYLUM

Amnesty International

Human rights violations arising from civil wars and ethnic conflicts in the 1990s have led to an increase in the worldwide refugee population, claims Amnesty International (AI) in the following viewpoint. Despite international laws that guarantee protection of refugees fleeing persecution, AI contends, emigrés seeking safety face an increasing number of barriers to political asylum. According to AI, these barriers include restrictive immigration measures, visa requirements, forced repatriation, and long-term detention. Amnesty International is a worldwide voluntary movement that works to prevent governmental violations of people's fundamental human rights.

As you read, consider the following questions:

1. According to Amnesty International, what is the difference between a refugee and a migrant?
2. What is the principle of non-refoulement, according to AI?
3. According to AI, what happened to Fauziya Kasinga when she sought asylum in the United States?

Reprinted from "Refugees: Human Rights Have No Borders," in Amnesty International Report 1997 (London: Amnesty International Publications, 1997), ISBN 1-887204-11-3, A.I. Index: POL 10/01/97, by permission.

In the 1980s, there were some eight million refugees worldwide. In the 1990s, the number of refugees seeking protection from terrible human rights violations has almost doubled: to more than 15 million. Refugees are people who have fled their countries because they have a well-founded fear of persecution and cannot rely on their own governments to protect them. This is what distinguishes refugees from other migrants. Increasingly these people are evidence of the extent to which persecution, mass human rights violations and abuses arising out of civil war and other conflicts have erupted around the world during the 1990s, leaving refugees in their wake.

WOMEN AND CHILDREN REFUGEES

Most of the world's refugees are women and children. The majority of them have fled for the same reasons as men. Some refugees, however, have been forced to leave their homes because of human rights violations and abuses directed primarily or solely at women. Women from zones of conflict have fled areas where soldiers have systematically raped and sexually abused young girls and women. In Afghanistan, the states of the former Yugoslavia, Zaire and other countries, rape was used to terrorize civilians into flight. Women have also sought asylum abroad because of fear of persecution due to the status or activities of male relatives, or because they have transgressed, or refuse to conform to, discriminatory religious, social or customary laws and practices. Some women have fled their countries to seek protection from the practice of female genital mutilation.

Women are not even safe once they have found refuge. In 1991, some 300,000 Somali refugees fled inter-clan fighting, famine and disease in their country. In 1996, some 170,000 Somali refugees were still living in Kenya. Most were housed in three camps in a remote area of the northeast, near the border with Somalia. Hundreds of Somali women were raped in these camps between April 1992 and November 1993. Although the majority of rapists were bandits, a number of women were raped by Kenyan soldiers or police. As far as Amnesty International is aware, to this day those responsible for raping or assaulting Somali refugees have not been brought to justice.

CRISES IN AFRICA AND EUROPE

The growing number of refugees is neither a temporary problem nor the random product of chance events. It is the predictable consequence of human rights crises throughout the world. Often these crises were foreseen. In the two years before the outbreak of genocidal violence in Rwanda, a United Nations (UN) human rights expert warned that unless states took determined action, mass killings would follow. The international community not only failed to heed these warnings, but, when the massacres started in April 1994, withdrew the UN troops. Since then, refugee crisis has followed refugee crisis in the region, with millions of men, women and children suffering dislocation, terror, disease, starvation and death. . . .

Decades of atrocities have set populations against each other in Africa's Great Lakes region. But the many disparate groups from Rwanda, Zaire and Burundi have one thing in common: they are in grave danger of continued human rights abuses and they are not getting from states and intergovernmental organizations the full protection which is due to refugees under regional and international treaties.

The refugee crisis in Europe also shows little sign of improvement. Its worst human rights disaster since the 1940s is far from being resolved. From 1991, as the former Yugoslavia fractured, systematic rape, mass murder and "disappearance" became commonplace. More than two million people in Bosnia and Herzegovina alone fled their homes, friends and livelihoods. Some found temporary refuge in Europe, others are still displaced within the country. One year after the peace agreement which brought an end to open conflict, there was little real progress towards establishing the durably safe conditions which would allow refugees and displaced people to return to their homes. . . .

NATIONS EVADE RESPONSIBILITY

The majority of the world's states have undertaken to accept and protect refugees fleeing persecution, by ratifying the 1951 UN Convention relating to the Status of Refugees (UN Refugee Convention) and its 1967 Protocol. However, more than 50 have not, and some of those sit on the Executive Committee of the UN High Commissioner for Refugees (UNHCR), the advisory body of the UNHCR. The Office of the UNHCR is the UN agency charged with protecting and assisting refugees.

Sudden mass movements of refugees often signal terror and human rights catastrophes. They should alert the international community to act swiftly to prevent further human rights tragedies and to develop coordinated strategies to protect and support refugees.

Instead, the 1990s have seen states take inadequate action to prevent the human rights violations which cause refugees to flee and at the same time evade their responsibilities towards refugees. Countries which proclaim the importance they attach to human rights simultaneously force men, women and children back into the arms of their persecutors by obstructing access to asylum procedures, misinterpreting the UN Refugee Convention definition of who is a refugee and forcibly returning those who are in need of protection.

The international regime that is supposed to protect refugees is in crisis. The UN Refugee Convention and its Protocol, which was designed to protect refugees fleeing persecution, often prove inadequate because many situations faced by refugees today are deemed to fall outside their terms. There is a gap in international protection for many of those who need it most. Many states have devised alternative legal categories in order to protect refugees, including "humanitarian status" and "de facto refugees". However, these categories are uncertain and usually mean that those in need of protection are given insufficient rights. The reasons why people flee their homes are becoming more complicated in a world beset by armed conflict, political instability and persecution of one nationality by another. . . .

The problems caused by inadequate protective measures are compounded by the fact that many states talk about the rights of refugees, while in practice devoting their energies to keeping refugees away from their borders, forcing them back into the arms of their persecutors and claiming that few who seek asylum are "real" refugees. States' commitment to offering asylum is dwindling, as is their political will to resolve the plight of desperate refugees, and minimal action is being taken to prevent the human rights violations which have caused people to flee their homes. . . .

REFOULEMENT

Increasingly, states are forcibly returning individuals to countries where their life or freedom is threatened—a practice known as refoulement. Refoulement is prohibited under Article 33 of the UN Refugee Convention and under other international instruments. The principle of non-refoulement is a fundamental one and is considered to be a norm of customary international law, which all states are obliged to uphold. Yet many states violate this obligation and return refugees to countries where they are at grave risk. . . .

The world's richest countries host the minority of the world's refugees. While accepting in theory the principle of non-refoulement, in practice "northern" states return refugees by employing a variety of legal and administrative measures to obstruct and deter refugees from seeking asylum. Defenders of the rights of refugees have lost some of the battles over policy. They are now losing individual cases as "northern" states put their increasingly restrictive policies into practice. In many countries, public opinion is swayed by portrayals of genuine refugees as "bogus" economic migrants or as lacking in credibility.

OFFICIAL REFUGEES, ASIA, AFRICA, AND EUROPE, 1980–93

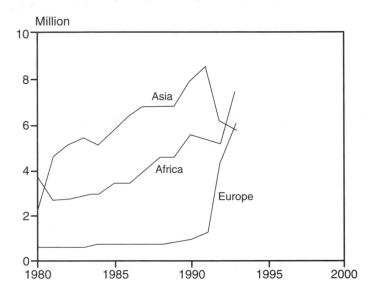

Source: United Nations High Commission for Refugees

"Northern" states avoid their obligations towards refugees by obstructing access. The measures used include rejection at the border, carrier sanctions, visa requirements that are impossible for asylum-seekers to fulfill, international zones in airports and interdiction at sea. For those refugees able to get into a country, the use of "safe third country" practices, "white lists", and readmission agreements result in refugees being sent to countries they may have travelled through, or to the country they fled. In Turkey, asylum-seekers have to register their claim within five days of entering the country. Asylum-seekers who failed to comply with the five-day rule have been returned to countries where they were at risk of serious human rights violations. Mehrdad, an Iranian citizen who was a member of the People's Mojahedin Organization of Iran (PMOI), spent 10 years in prison in Iran and was subjected to torture. He was released, but fled to Turkey in August 1995 because he feared rearrest. UNHCR recognized his asylum claim, but in April the Turkish authorities forcibly returned him to Iran for having failed to register his asylum claim within five days of arrival. On his return to Iran he was arrested and interrogated. Worldwide appeals on his behalf flooded in from Amnesty International members and other organizations. Mehrdad was eventually released after agreeing to return to Turkey and to send letters to the UN and human rights organizations criticizing the PMOI. Once in Turkey, he escaped from Iranian officials accompanying him and again sought asylum. He was eventually resettled in another country.

"Safe Third Countries"

Some "northern" states off-load their obligations by sending asylum-seekers to a "safe third country". Sometimes the only connection the asylum-seeker has with the country is that their plane stopped to refuel there. Many "third countries" are far from safe; some do not adhere to the international refugee treaties, let alone have they established adequate mechanisms for dealing with asylum-seekers. One such country is Pakistan. Hundreds of thousands of refugees from civil war and mass human rights violations in Afghanistan have crossed the border to Pakistan in search of safety. However, many of them remained at risk there. Prominent Afghans living in Pakistan have frequently been targeted for assassination and abduction.

Mariam Azimi, an Afghan asylum-seeker, was forced to hide in a church in Norway with her two young children because the authorities did not believe her when she said it was unsafe for her to be sent to Pakistan. Already vulnerable by virtue of being an educated Afghan woman, she was in particular danger in Afghanistan because she had campaigned for women's rights. After receiving repeated death threats, she fled to Pakistan, where she continued her campaigning. She was again threatened by Afghan Mojahedin groups who operate in border areas in Pakistan. Attempts were made to kill members of her family and she was forced yet again to flee in fear of her life. She arrived in Norway with her two young children in search of asylum. The authorities rejected her claim on the grounds that it was safe for her to return to Pakistan. She went into hiding with her children to escape being forcibly repatriated.

Carrier Sanctions

Many "northern" states continue to impose carrier sanctions, whereby fines are imposed on shipowners and airlines that allow people without the required paperwork to board their craft. These sanctions can have terrifying consequences.

In May 1996, three Romanian asylum-seekers who had stowed away on a container ship were left to drown off the coast of Canada after being forced off the Taiwanese ship *Mersk Dubai* into the sea. According to members of the ship's crew, they were given no life jackets, just pieces of styrofoam which were tied round their waists. The asylum-seekers did not have the proper papers, and the shipping company could have been fined $6,000 per person if the captain had landed them in Canada. A crew member said that he saw the stowaways pleading for their lives as the ship's officers forced them to climb down the ladder and into the ocean.

Immigration officials from "northern" countries have been dispatched to countries which produce large numbers of refugees to show airline staff how to spot passengers with suspect papers or motives. Airlines conduct pre-flight screenings at points of embarkation, especially at airports where potential asylum-seekers are expected. In Nairobi, Kenya, for example, Dutch and British immigration officials have trained airline staff in recognizing fraudulent travel documents. In several European Union member states, airline staff have the power to decide whether travel documents are genuine, despite the European Parliament resolution of 24 September 1995 that all asylum-seekers should have automatic and unfettered access to admission procedures, and that visa policies and sanctions on carriers should not be an impediment to such access. Measures which obstruct the entry of asylum-seekers, including visa requirements and carrier sanctions, are incompatible with the object and purpose of the international system for the protection of refugees. People fleeing persecution will often not be able to obtain the proper travel documents and may have no choice but to flee with false documentation.

CHANGES IN RULES

Some states are trying to evade their responsibilities towards asylum-seekers while their claims are being assessed. A Zairian woman, Ms B., traumatized after being raped by state officials, arrived in the United Kingdom in February, hoping to find asylum. She arrived just a few days after a rule change which meant that only those who applied for asylum immediately at the port of entry were eligible to receive welfare payments while their claims were assessed.

Ms B. had been arrested in Zaire at a memorial meeting for her husband, who had been shot dead during an anti-government rally. In prison, she had been repeatedly raped by guards. A guard finally took pity on her and smuggled her out in a sack. Her family paid for her to travel to the United Kingdom via Belgium. She arrived in London by train and then went directly to the Home Office, some kilometres away, where she applied for asylum. She was subsequently denied any welfare payments on the grounds that she had not submitted her asylum application immediately on arrival at the port of entry. A legal challenge was made to the Court of Appeal, which in June ruled in her favour. One of the judges stated:

> A significant number of genuine asylum-seekers now find themselves faced with a bleak choice: whether to remain here destitute and homeless until their claims are finally determined or whether instead to abandon their claims and return to face the very persecution they have fled.

This legal victory was short-lived. In July 1996, the British parliament passed legislation denying welfare payments to all those who failed to apply for asylum immediately on arrival and to people appealing against rejection of their asylum claim. However, in October a new High Court ruling required local government authorities to provide some assistance to asylum-seekers. In December, for the first time in 50 years, the Red Cross distributed food parcels in London. The recipients were destitute asylum-seekers.

In September 1996, legislation limiting the social benefits available to immigrants and some refugees also came into force in the United States of America (USA).

DETAINING ASYLUM-SEEKERS

The international community has agreed that states should normally avoid detaining asylum-seekers. However, in Europe and North America the use of detention has increased dramatically as states make strenuous efforts to deter and obstruct refugees from seeking asylum in their countries. In some countries, such as the USA and Austria, some asylum-seekers are detained as soon as they arrive and are held while their applications are processed. In many countries, refugees are held in the transit zones of international airports and then expelled. In others, specific groups of asylum-seekers are placed behind bars—for example, those whose applications are considered "unfounded". In a recent study, "Cell Culture", Amnesty International's United Kingdom Section examined the cases of 150 of 700 asylum-seekers detained in the United Kingdom and highlighted the arbitrariness of detention of asylum-seekers in the country. Asylum-seekers are sometimes detained for years while they await a decision on their case, although they have committed no crime. . . .

PUNISHMENT WITHOUT CRIME

The arbitrary detention of asylum-seekers and refugees is punishment without crime. Depriving asylum-seekers of their liberty puts many in exactly the situation they fled to escape and makes it much more difficult for them to pursue their asylum claims.

Asylum-seekers in the USA are often held in remote locations, given inaccurate information about their status, and shackled hand and foot during asylum hearings; some have been held in cruel, inhuman or degrading conditions. Fauziya Kasinga was hit with a stick, sprayed with tear-gas and kicked at the detention centre where she was sent after seeking asylum in the USA. She had fled to escape female genital mutilation in her home country of Togo. When she arrived in the USA, she immediately asked for asylum and was taken to Esmor Detention Centre in handcuffs and shackles. Conditions in Esmor were harsh, with poor food, lack of heat, insect-infested bedding, filthy clothing and theft of detainees' belongings by staff. Fauziya, just 17 years old, was detained for more than a year in various detention centres. In April, she was finally granted asylum on the recognition that women fleeing persecution in the form of genital mutilation are refugees deserving international protection. . . .

REFUGEE PROTECTION WOULD PREVENT VIOLATIONS

Amnesty International works to prevent the human rights violations which cause people to flee their homes. It opposes the return of any person to a country where he or she would be at risk of serious human rights violations, such as imprisonment as a prisoner of conscience, torture, execution or "disappearance". This is the basis of Amnesty International's work for refugees. It is an important element of preventive human rights work—acting to prevent abuses, not just responding after they have occurred. Amnesty International calls on governments to ensure that their asylum procedures meet minimum international standards of fairness, impartiality and thoroughness. A corollary is that Amnesty International demands that no asylum-seeker is forcibly expelled without having had his or her claim properly examined. The organization also calls on governments to ensure that they do not expel someone to a country which may itself forcibly return refugees to danger.

Human rights activists campaigning on behalf of refugees

face a dual challenge at the international level. They must uphold the protection provided by international refugee law in the face of growing efforts by governments to avoid and circumvent their obligations. They must also strive to ensure that as the world throws up new challenges to human rights, the system of international protection is extended to meet those challenges.

| "Driven by emotional impulse and
perceived national obligations, . . .
humanitarian intake [of refugees]
has escaped rational management."

MANY CLAIMS OF REFUGEE STATUS ARE UNWARRANTED

David Simcox

In the following viewpoint, David Simcox argues that the manageability of the U.S. population is threatened by an uncontrolled influx of immigrants claiming political refugee status. In recent years, Simcox contends, the definition of persecuted groups has been extended to include women in male-dominated societies, homosexuals, Chinese people of reproductive age, and various religious minorities. According to Simcox, this enlarged definition of persecuted groups—as well as the lax screening of potential political asylees—has allowed too many immigrants into the United States on the basis of unwarranted or false claims of refugee status. Simcox is the director of research of Negative Population Growth, an organization that works to promote a decrease in U.S. and world populations.

As you read, consider the following questions:

1. In the United States, what is the difference between a refugee and an asylee, according to Simcox?
2. According to the author, how many aliens have gained residence in the United States by claiming the need for asylum?
3. What three steps should be taken to reform political asylum, in Simcox's opinion?

Reprinted from David Simcox, "Political Asylum: Achilles' Heel of Immigration Control," NPG Forum, November 1995, by permission of Negative Population Growth, Inc.

Immigration of 1.1 million persons a year perpetuates population growth and dims prospects for a smaller, environmentally sustainable U.S. population. Since the 1970s the vast majority of Americans have voted by their fertility rates to stabilize population. But immigration has nullified their choice. Humanitarian immigration—refugees, asylees and temporarily protected persons—has swollen to more than one-quarter of all immigration. Often driven by emotional impulse and perceived national obligations, and unlimited by law, humanitarian intake has escaped rational management.

Political asylum is the most idealistic, most uncontrollable, and most poorly managed of all features of the country's convoluted immigration rules. As envisioned in the 1980 Refugee Act, asylum offers safe haven to persons already in the United States or at a port of entry who can show a well-founded fear of persecution in their countries for reasons of race, ethnicity, religion, political opinion or associations.

The criterion of persecution is the same for asylum seekers here and refugees abroad. But a key practical distinction between refugees and asylees under present arrangements is that the United States chooses from abroad the refugees it will resettle; with political asylum, the United States passively allows itself to be chosen by hundreds of thousands of international migrants, many driven by motives other than refuge.

A WORLD-WIDE LURE

As now applied, U.S. asylum laws proclaim to the globe's 5.5 billion non-Americans that if they can somehow enter the United States and claim persecution within their homelands, they will be able to live and work here for many months, if not years, during the slow paced adjudication of their claims. An attraction not lost on millions abroad is that even among those ultimately denied asylum, few are removed from the United States.

In 1992, 45 percent of asylum claimants failed to appear for their initial hearing; they simply took the work authorization card granted by the Immigration Service (INS) and disappeared into U.S. society. Others go through the hearings process, but drop out of sight if asylum is denied. The government now has neither the means nor will to track them down. Other applicants acquire U.S. spouses and citizen children during the lengthy process, making their removal harder. Small wonder then that the system has become an enormous magnet for hundreds of thousands of would-be settlers who cannot qualify under regular immigration rules or are unwilling to wait in line for a visa.

The asylum system is subverted by interest groups' skillful manipulation, by often uninformed compassion among Americans, and by the extreme and unworkable definition of "due process" that asylum's advocates have fastened upon it. An article of faith among immigration advocates is that there can never be too much due process. An allied assumption is that it is better that thousands of spurious claimants receive asylum than one bona fide claimant be denied it.

Thus the system sets itself up to be manipulated by hundreds of thousands. The asylum applicant enjoys far more due process than is required by international obligations or by the U.S. constitution. Prospective refugees abroad have far fewer rights. Court decisions, unchallenged by the executive branch, have expanded the definition of persecution and further reduced the evidentiary burden on the asylum claimant. A history of inconsistent policies, capitulations to interest group demands, and unfounded presumptions have created grounds for expansive rulings in the federal courts.

The scope of asylum's protection has been extended to new allegedly persecuted classes: homosexuals; women in male-dominated societies, or who are victims of spousal abuse, or who are from societies where female circumcision is practiced; and persons claiming to flee China's family limitation laws. Efforts to protect more and more victim classes are as often driven by domestic political wrangling over issues such as women's and gay rights, or right to life, as they are humanitarian reactions to events abroad. An underlying fallacy that makes asylum open-ended is the assumption of its defenders that the Western yardstick on human rights must be applied to the entire crowded and impoverished world.

A SUBSTANTIAL POPULATION FACTOR

Political asylum, as now legislated, is truly an "Achilles' Heel"—an inherently vulnerable and unmanageable feature of U.S. immigration policy that is the antithesis of the discipline and rationality needed to manage immigration in accord with sound population goals.

The current law's 10,000 ceiling on the number of asylees granted legal permanent residence each year far understates the program's much larger impact on population. Most asylum claimants manage to stay, with or without the blessing of the "green card," the talisman of legal permanent residents. Though the number actually granted formal asylum is far lower, nearly 500,000 aliens outside the legal immigration process now have gained legal or *de facto* permanent residence with the help of their access to the asylum channel. In 1993 and 1994 the pool of those admitted for asylum claims grew by nearly 100,000 each year. Uncounted others now living illegally in the United States, but who have not yet claimed asylum, were emboldened to remain here by the availability of the asylum defense if needed to ward off deportation. . . .

UNDERMINING ASYLUM

The legitimacy of the refugee/asylum concept is being undermined by a legal loophole that the immigration lobby, expansive-minded immigration judges, and the current administration have used to dramatically increase the types of persons granted asylum.

Instead of being restricted to a few basic categories widely supported by the American public (such as persons fleeing Communist regimes) successful asylum-seekers now include such groups as:

* Homosexuals claiming governmental or societal persecution
* HIV/AIDS sufferers hoping to gain access to American health care
* Feminists or upper-class educated women from male-dominated societies
* Chinese nationals objecting to their government's one-child-family policy
* Practitioners of transcendental meditation.

James S. Robb, *Social Contract,* Summer 1997.

The prudent assumption must be that the asylum system, without radical reforms, will become an even larger conduit for extra-legal immigration in the future. Rapid world population growth and deteriorating environments will produce millions of new candidates abroad for entry by any means.

THE TRAP OF DEFINITIONS

The current expansive definition of persecution opens up the prospect of vast new categories of claimants in a world increasingly given to ethnic and religious divisions. Some legislators would by law make China's mandatory abortion and sterilization policies a legal basis for asylum, opening the door to millions of Chinese of reproductive age and their children. Sponsors of the legislation themselves note that a "few million men, women and children" now suffer from China's policy.

The spread of an intolerant Islamic fundamentalism bodes vast new asylum claims from liberal Moslems, non-believers, Christians and other religious minorities in the Moslem world. At the same time, the rise of militant fundamentalist Hinduism in overcrowded India carries the potential to convert that nation's 100 million Moslems into a persecuted class. The emphasis on human rights for women has the potential to make countless women in the third world eligible for asylum claims, since their home countries have gender-based customs that they—and western societies—find increasingly difficult to accept.

Current efforts in Congress to reduce legal immigration and end illegal immigration, even if partly successful, will heighten the attractiveness of the asylum gateway for desperate would-be settlers. The recent experience of Germany, where asylum was a constitutional right, dramatizes the explosive growth potential of a lax system. There, asylum claims surged from about 50,000 a year in 1987 to over 400,000 a year in 1992 before the German government applied tough restrictions.

The abuse of the current asylum system mocks the good faith applicants for immigration who wait to enter the United States by the rules. Public support for the needs of genuine refugees suffers in the process. This uncontrollable immigration valve confounds rational immigration planning, saps the credibility of U.S. immigration controls, and invites greater mass influxes in the future.

THREE STEPS TO REFORM ASYLUM

If asylum is to cease being the wild card of immigration control, it must be reformed in three general aspects.

First, asylum's value as an alternative route to permanent settlement must be ended by making all grants of asylum temporary only. This would "demagnetize" asylum as an easy way to circumvent legal immigration limits while still helping those truly at risk.

Second, the flow of claimants through the asylum pipeline, now potentially unlimited, must be restricted by far more judicious selection of cases to be considered. While Congress is now considering major increases in the number of asylum officers, huge backlogs, with the attendant danger of "rubber stamping," are likely as long as we pretend that everyone capable of reaching U.S. shores is entitled to his day(s) in court.

Third, the United States must show the world that it will no longer allow its laws to be "gamed." Those applications for asylum that are accepted for adjudication must be decided quickly, followed by the prompt removal from the country of those rejected. More convincing would be a decision deadline of no more than 60 days, rather than the 120 days the INS has adopted. The President was vague about when action would begin on the plan he announced in May, 1995, to triple deportations from the present 40,000 a year.

Sustained deportations of 120,000 a year, once the priority target of criminal aliens has been removed, would greatly reduce the pool of overstays, no-shows, and prospective abusers abroad by either timely removal or by the credible threat of it.

PROPOSALS FOR ACTION

Here are some specific actions for consideration by policy makers that would support the three general objectives outlined above. Most are drawn from proposals already made in the U.S. government or in other industrial nations:

• *Grant asylum for a temporary stay only, ending it when conditions are satisfactory in a country where the asylee has a right to reside.* The present practice of granting successful asylum claimants "green cards" is a powerful attraction to economic migrants. Conflict and instability in such countries as Lebanon, Central America, Ethiopia, Poland, and the former Soviet Union brought new waves of political asylees to the United States in the 1970s and 1980s. Most have remained as permanent residents, often joined by relatives from abroad, even though peace and stability have returned to their home countries.

The purpose of asylum should be to protect the truly persecuted rather than to resettle them. The United States should follow a practice of some other western democratic countries in making grants of asylum only for the duration of the conditions abroad that motivated flight. Decisions of U.S. officials to extend or terminate asylum would be based on yearly reviews of conditions in asylees' home countries. Supporting this would be continuing U.S. diplomatic efforts to persuade sending countries to accept returnees, foreswear persecution of them, and even accept international monitoring if necessary.

Family members would be admitted to live with asylees in the United States only if they independently established a well-founded fear of persecution in their own right. Although considered temporary admissions, asylee numbers should still be subject to an overall annual ceiling on all forms of immigration. Those granted asylum should be charged to the ceiling when their stay exceeds one year. Those numbers could be restored to the ceiling upon confirmation of the permanent departure of the asylees.

PREVENTING "ASYLUM SHOPPING"

• *Reject outright all applications for asylum from persons with the rights of residence or sojourn in a country classified by the U.S. government as having adequate human rights protections.* The Justice Department now wastes immense resources in processing cases of persons from countries that have satisfactory human rights standards. Often these claimants are "asylum shoppers" seeking the best deal, economic migrants, or persons who have not exhausted their legal remedies in their home countries.

A list of countries with adequate human rights standards should be developed by the Justice and State Departments and updated periodically. Asylum claims from persons eligible to reside or sojourn in those countries would no longer be entertained. The absence of any country from the list, however, would in no way be considered a presumption that asylum is warranted. Strict standards of proof of individual persecution would continue to apply.

Many countries now grant passports without the stringent requirements of nationality applied by the United States. Aliens with a passport from a country other than the one they allege to be fleeing would be presumed to have accepted the protection of the issuing country and would be repatriated there.

These examples from asylum adjudication of the past ten years illustrate how such an approach would prevent unjustified claims from tying up the system:

1. The case of an asylum applicant from Northern Ireland claiming to fear Irish Republican Army (IRA) violence was under adjudication for several years. Under the proposed approach, her asylum claim would have been summarily rejected because she had the right to reside in the United Kingdom or the Republic of Ireland, both of which have adequate human rights protections.

2. A Somalian and his family claimed asylum at the airport during transit through New York after passing through at least two safe countries, the United Kingdom and Italy. To justify transiting the United States, the family had obtained valid visas to enter Brazil. Under the proposal, the claimants would have been sent on to Brazil, a country with satisfactory human rights that they had permission to enter.

3. A migrant from apartheid-ruled South Africa flew to New York from Spain, where he had been granted political asylum.

He applied for asylum in the U.S., was detained and entered the adjudication system. Under the proposed approach, after appropriate interviews he would have been returned immediately to Spain, a satisfactory human rights country.

4. Afghan asylum seekers in the 1980s often traveled on Pakistani passports to the United States to claim asylum. Under these proposals, no claims for asylum would have been accepted and the travelers would have been returned to Pakistan, whose protection they had accepted.

The prompt rejection of applicants from countries known to be safe would curb "asylum shopping," deter frivolous requests, and spare Justice Department resources for higher enforcement priorities. . . .

REMOVING FALSE CLAIMANTS

• *Quickly remove applicants who have used false documents or otherwise entered illegally.* Congress and the administration are now considering several variants of a process of immediate removal of claimants who have entered surreptitiously or are document abusers and who are determined in an interview with asylum officers not to have a "credible fear" of persecution. The test of "credible fear" in these and all other cases should be more stringent than in the past, requiring the asylum officer's finding that "persecution would be more probable than not" if the claimant were sent home.

Persons entering illegally often do not claim asylum until detected and faced with removal. Limiting applications for asylum to a short period after entry or after the presumably threatening political event in the home country would discourage use of the process as a stall. Article 31 of the Geneva Convention on Refugees states that aliens entering a country to claim refugee status must "present themselves without delay to the authorities and show good cause for their illegal entry or presence."

Deserving support is a congressional proposal that an alien must state his intent to seek asylum within thirty days after coming to the United States. Aliens who fail to appear for hearings without good cause—a common occurrence—should have their applications summarily dismissed and be subject to immediate removal. . . .

U.S. RHETORIC ANIMATES MILLIONS ABROAD

Since George Washington's time, U.S. political leaders' rhetoric has regularly proclaimed the United States as a haven for the world's downtrodden. It is high time to realize that these self-congratulatory incantations are taken very seriously abroad. A related complication has been the notion in the cold war years that huge inflows of people of an adversary nation somehow represent a diplomatic victory.

BLANKET REFUGEE STATUS?

President Jimmy Carter greeted the initial waves of Mariel boat people in the 1980s with the words, "We'll continue to provide an open heart and open arms to refugees seeking freedom from communist domination," even as U.S. agencies were struggling to slow the flow of boat people. The 1966 Cuban Adjustment Act had helped create a magnet, offering blanket refugee status to Cubans reaching the United States. That cold war measure remains on the books: it stands as a threat to rational control of the Cuban influx that must be expected when travel controls end on the island, and as an incentive to other emigre groups to seek similar preferential treatment.

Congress in the 1970s and 1980s applied pressure on the Soviet Union through such devices as the 1974 Jackson-Vanek trade sanctions act to allow freer emigration. The Clinton administration even now continues to press China to allow more emigration, echoing a similar appeal of President Carter during Chinese Vice Premier Deng Xiaoping's 1979 visit to the United States. (Deng's response: "Are you prepared to accept ten million?")

Even faint and confused signals about immigration from U.S. leaders spur movement abroad. In June 1995, a House of Representatives bill to deter the UN-planned voluntary repatriation of 40,000 refugees in Hong Kong set off riots, caused thousands of refugees to try to renege, and risked sparking a new exodus from Vietnam. Similarly, Presidential candidate Bill Clinton's 1991 pledge to end the Bush administration's interdiction of Haitian boat people sparked a major surge of boat building within Haiti.

IN THE NATIONAL INTEREST

Taming the familiar political rituals of more than two centuries must come as part of a new American appreciation of the limits of U.S. society and resources and the dangers of leaving migration choices to the migrants themselves. Every question of how many to admit is at heart a question about how many Americans there will be in the future.

An America already overpopulated in relation to its resources must make these choices within the limits set by an overall population policy—a careful balancing of fertility, mortality and immigration that will permit the U.S. population to recede toward a sustainable level in the twenty-first century.

The message America must now send abroad is not an open invitation to scores of millions more, but an affirmation of its commitment to bring its own population size down to the limits of the nation's and the planet's life supports. Limitation of political asylum is central in that message.

"Every 22 minutes, someone loses a limb or a life to a land mine—more than 26,000 men, women and children each year."

THE USE OF LAND MINES VIOLATES HUMAN RIGHTS

Karen J. Longstreth

Land mines—buried explosive devices intended to wound or kill enemy soldiers who trigger them—cause thousands of civilian casualties each year, argues Karen J. Longstreth in the following viewpoint. In many parts of the world, Longstreth points out, land mines remain in the ground long after the resolution of armed conflicts, maiming and killing innocent people. She contends that an international ban on the use of land mines would prevent such needless injury and death. Longstreth is a member of the United Nations Association, a nonprofit research organization dedicated to strengthening U.S. participation in the United Nations.

As you read, consider the following questions:

1. What is the average life span of a land mine, according to Longstreth?
2. According to the author, which countries contain high numbers of leftover land mines?
3. How does the cost of making land mines compare with the cost of removing them, according to Longstreth?

Reprinted from Karen Longstreth, "A World Where No One Fears Walking," *San Diego Union-Tribune*, May 16, 1997, by permission of the author.

I magine being afraid of where you walk—that the next step you take could cost you a foot, both legs or your life.

We Americans worry about crime and overcrowded schools, Medicare cuts and air pollution, television violence and freeway congestion. But there probably isn't a single American who hesitates to walk outside in the yard or neighborhood for fear of being blown to bits by a land mine. It's almost unimaginable.

However, people in at least 68 less fortunate nations worry about their next step. In these countries, there are an estimated 110 million uncleared mines lying in fields, deserts, roads, forests and waterways. Every 22 minutes, someone loses a limb or a life to a land mine—more than 26,000 men, women and children each year.

A Continuing Threat

Anti-personnel (AP) mines, so-called because they are designed to kill or maim the person who triggers them, do not discriminate between the foot of a soldier and the foot of a child at play. Land mines do not recognize peace accords or cease-fires. With an average life span of 50 to 100 years, they lie in hiding for decades after hostilities have ceased.

Most of the victims are civilians, often women and children. Children are especially vulnerable because they are often closer to the center of the blast, and their survival chances after massive blood loss are minimal.

Land mines are a daily threat in many countries where the number of leftover mines is particularly staggering: Afghanistan (10 million), Angola (15 million), Bosnia (3 million), Cambodia (10 million), Croatia (3 million), Iraq (10 million), Mozambique (2 million), Somalia (1 million) and Vietnam (3.5 million). In Cambodia, there are more than 35,000 amputees; one of every 200 Cambodians has lost one or more limbs to a land-mine explosion. The manufacture of artificial limbs is one of the few growth industries in some countries.

In the United States, many of those most familiar with land mines are in wheelchairs or Veterans Administration hospitals. Land mines caused 33 percent of all U.S. casualties and 28 percent of all deaths in Vietnam. In the Persian Gulf War, 34 percent of U.S. casualties were attributed to mines. The first U.S. soldiers to die in Vietnam and Bosnia were killed by AP mines. An especially sad irony is that the U.S. Army estimates that 90 percent of land mines and booby traps used against U.S. troops in Vietnam were either U.S. made or included U.S. made components.

During the last 25 years, approximately 50 nations have produced and exported about 200 million AP mines. The United States, China, Italy and the former Soviet Union have been the leading producers. Not only are land mines widely considered the cruelest and least discriminating weapons of war, they are some of the cheapest. They cost as little as $3 to $15 to make.

LAND MINES

Eleanor Mill. Reprinted by permission of Mill NewsArt Syndicate.

On the other hand, mine removal and clearance programs are painstakingly slow, dangerous and expensive. The United Nations estimates a cost of $300 to $1,000 to remove each one, a huge financial burden for the world's poorest nations. According to a United Nations Association fact sheet, 100,000 mines are cleared per year. At that rate, if mine proliferation were stopped now, it would take 1,100 years to remove mines currently in the ground.

In 1992, an international coalition of humanitarian and

human-rights groups, including Human Rights Watch (U.S.), Handicap International (France) and the Vietnam Veterans of America Foundation, launched a campaign to bring attention to the global land-mine crisis. Its goal was a comprehensive ban on the production, trade, stockpiling and use of land mines.

After five years, this campaign grew to over 1,000 non-government organizations in 50 countries, including the United States. Here, over 200 groups have enlisted in the U.S. Campaign to Ban Landmines. The United Nations Association—USA—is one of these organizations.

Retired Gen. Norman Schwarzkopf, Pope John Paul II and Archbishop Desmond Tutu have also endorsed a complete ban. To date, 156 nations are on record in support of the ban. Representatives of many of them plan to sign a legally binding international treaty in Ottawa in December 1997.

U.S. POLICY ON LAND MINES

What is the present U.S. policy? Where does President Clinton stand? On May 16, 1996, the president stated, "Today I am launching an international effort to ban anti-personnel land mines. . . . The United States will lead a global effort to eliminate these terrible weapons and to stop the enormous loss of human life."

Since his statement, the president has taken a detour by choosing to negotiate the ban through the U.N. Conference on Disarmament rather than joining over 50 countries, including major North Atlantic Treaty Organization (NATO) allies, in signing the ban treaty in Canada. Negotiations in the Conference on Disarmament are notoriously slow and usually measured in decades.

On May 16, 1997, President Clinton was reminded of his words when hundreds of people gathered across from the White House to urge him to keep his promise. Petitions with over 100,000 signatures were presented from Americans demanding a land-mine ban. There were also 26,000 shoes to remind the president of as many people worldwide who had lost a leg or a life to a mine in the year since he had promised a ban.

The U.S. Campaign to Ban Landmines urges you to take action today as well. Contact the president and your representatives in Congress. Ask them to urge the U.S. government to sign the international ban treaty, to legislate a permanent ban on production, trade and use of AP land mines, and to increase support for humanitarian mine clearance and victim-assistance programs.

We should ban land-mine use as a step toward enabling all the world's people to walk without fear.

| "Trying to outlaw mines is much like trying to outlaw war itself, an exercise in futility."

OUTLAWING LAND MINES WOULD BE FUTILE

Bernard E. Trainor

Many human rights activists contend that a global ban on the use of land mines is needed to prevent the civilian injuries and deaths presently caused by the devices. Bernard E. Trainor takes issue with this argument in the following viewpoint. He maintains that an international ban on land mines would not keep armed forces from using them. Furthermore, he points out, many modern armies actually use sophisticated mines that automatically deactivate after a short time, thereby minimizing the threat to innocent civilians. A global ban on land mines could put American troops at a disadvantage by disallowing the use of these sophisticated mines, he asserts. Trainor, a retired marine lieutenant general, directs the national security program at Harvard's Kennedy School of Government.

As you read, consider the following questions:

1. For what reason does Trainor feel ambivalent about the use of land mines?
2. How can soldiers make their own land mines, according to the author?
3. According to Trainor, which armed forces use land mines as a primary weapon?

Reprinted from Bernard E. Trainor, "Land Mines Saved My Life," New York Times, March 28, 1996, by permission. Copyright ©1996 by The New York Times Company.

In March 1952, I was making my way down Hill 59 in Korea, not far from the ongoing peace negotiations at Panmunjom. But there was no peace on the hill. After a brisk firefight the previous night, my platoon had taken the hill from Chinese Communist forces. Despite my caution, I tripped on a wire. I heard a "thip" as it activated a mine, and I steeled myself for the explosion that would rip off my legs. Nothing happened. The mine had malfunctioned.

Two nights later, the Chinese tried to recapture Hill 59. Anticipating this, my platoon had installed mines to protect our position. As mortar shells rained down and automatic-weapons fire swept the hill, I could hear mines detonating and shrieks of agony. The mines saved us from being overrun.

To this day, I cannot walk across an open field without an eerie feeling that death lurks in the tranquillity. Yet I feel ambivalent about mines. I know they have both threatened and saved my life.

U.S. TROOPS OFTEN DEPEND ON MINES

Senator Patrick J. Leahy, Democrat of Vermont, is sponsoring legislation that would forbid our military to use land mines. Supporters say such a ban could help lead to an international agreement to outlaw mines. The Senator is right to condemn the civilian deaths caused by leftover mines. And putting restrictions on international sales is a worthy goal that could save lives.

But we cannot wave a magic wand and do away with mines entirely. American troops often depend on them, and an international ban would not prevent other forces from using them. They will always be a trump card for troops who find themselves disadvantaged on the battlefield—and this, from time to time, includes Americans.

Unlike chemical weapons, to which Senator Leahy often compares them, mines are easy to make. In the early days of the Vietnam War, the Vietcong used trip wires to convert unexploded bombs and artillery shells into mines. Soldiers can fashion them from hand grenades or even pieces of pipe. For the most part, they do this not out of indifference to civilian lives but in the belief that it will save their own lives.

THE REAL PROBLEM

The world's modern armies have strict regulations, intended to protect civilians, governing the use of mines. Most have sophisticated mines that automatically deactivate in a few weeks or months. The real problem is the irregular troops, such as those in the former Yugoslavia, that use the devices indiscriminately as a principal weapon. Such forces would not be deterred by a ban but could find themselves with an advantage in a conflict with Americans.

AN IMPORTANT MILITARY TOOL

Banning the use of illegal "dumb mines" is laudable. Indiscriminately placed and incapable of self-destruction, these unmarked mines are continually responsible for civilian casualties. However, a global ban that would include "smart mines" will not help to solve the humanitarian problem. Smart mines automatically deactivate after prescribed periods of time. They are used in accordance with international laws of warfare, and are laid in well-marked areas threatened by hostile military forces—not in civilian areas. Such mines have proven to be an effective deterrent to aggression against U.S. forces or their allies.

U.S. Army doctrine recognizes the effectiveness of smart mines in protecting U.S. forces and denying terrain to an attacking enemy. In certain scenarios, the Army estimates that the proper use of smart anti-personnel land mines could cut American casualties in half by reducing the mobility of opposing forces and offering an effective early warning against attack. The responsible use of such mines, when deployed against an attacking military force, will save U.S. lives and not endanger civilians.

Baker Spring and John Hillen, Heritage Foundation *Executive Memorandum*, January 17, 1997.

Wars are terrible, and innocent people suffer from them even after they end. Artillery shells from World War I still take lives in Flanders. We may deplore the carnage, but it is a sad reality.

Trying to outlaw mines is much like trying to outlaw war itself, an exercise in futility. An international agreement restricting their sale might help protect civilians, but not letting our troops use them could cost American lives.

PERIODICAL BIBLIOGRAPHY

The following articles have been selected to supplement the diverse views presented in this chapter. Addresses are provided for periodicals not indexed in the *Readers' Guide to Periodical Literature*, the *Alternative Press Index*, the *Social Sciences Index*, or the *Index to Legal Periodicals and Books*.

Marshall Berman	"Modernism and Human Rights Near the Millennium," *Dissent*, Summer 1995.
Alan Cooperman	"The Creeping Return of the Soviet System," *U.S. News & World Report*, February 26, 1996.
Anton Foek	"Sweatshop Barbie: Exploitation of Third World Labor," *Humanist*, January/February 1997.
William J. Holstein et al.	"Santa's Sweatshop," *U.S. News & World Report*, December 16, 1996.
Journal of International Affairs	Issue on refugees and international population flows, Winter 1994.
Julie Light	"Baiting Immigrants: Women Bear the Brunt," *Progressive*, September 1996.
Pradeep S. Mehta	"Cashing In on Child Labor," *Multinational Monitor*, April 1994.
Aryeh Neier	"The New Double Standard," *Foreign Policy*, Winter 1996–1997.
Kathleen Newland	"Refugees: The Rising Flood," *World Watch*, May/June 1994.
Eyal Press	"Clinton Pushes Military Aid: Human-Rights Abusers Lap It Up," *Progressive*, February 1997.
James S. Robb	"Asylum *Ad Absurdum*," *Social Contract*, Summer 1997. Available from 316½ E. Mitchell St., Petoskey, MI 49770.
Jim Wurst	"Closing In on a Landmine Ban: The Ottawa Process and U.S. Interests," *Arms Control Today*, June/July 1997. Available from 1726 M St. NW, Suite 201, Washington, DC 20036.

CHAPTER 3

WHAT SHOULD BE DONE TO STOP HUMAN RIGHTS ABUSES?

Chapter Preface

At age four, Iqbal Masih of Pakistan was sold to the owner of a carpet factory and forced to work chained to a loom for up to sixteen hours a day, six days a week. When he was ten, Iqbal escaped from the factory and began a campaign protesting the exploitation of Pakistani children by the carpetmaking, garment, and brickmaking industries. Iqbal's activism earned him the 1994 Reebok Human Rights Award and a future scholarship to an American university, but in April 1995, at the age of twelve, he was murdered.

Iqbal's life has inspired many organizations, consumer groups, businesses, and individuals to contest the use of child labor. Canadian Craig Kielburger was twelve when he learned of Iqbal's story and began researching the issue of working children. In an article printed in the December 15, 1996, Chicago Tribune, Kielburger states that before reading about Masih, "I did not know very much about where my running shoes or soccer balls were made, or who made them. . . . Poor children in many countries are employed in the textile, sporting goods and toy industries, making products that may eventually end up on the shelves of North American stores. By buying these products, we may be contributing to the exploitation of children." With a group of friends, Kielburger launched Free the Children, an organization that urges consumers to learn about the origin and assembly of goods and to buy child-labor-free products. In a similar vein, in 1992, Democratic senator Tom Harkin first introduced the Child Labor Deterrence Act, a congressional bill that would ban imports made by children. Through such efforts, many human rights activists hope to stop the abuse and exploitation of children working in third world factories.

Some activists caution, however, that humanitarian challenges to the use of child labor can backfire. For example, 50,000 Bangladeshi children garment workers lost their jobs in 1993 after news of the Harkin bill aired. Many of these children then took on more dangerous work in the underground sex industry to make ends meet. To avoid such scenarios, many activist organizations do not support the boycott of goods made by children. Instead, they demand safe and humane working conditions for children along with a serious examination of the socioeconomic conditions that require young children to work.

The following chapter presents further debate about various approaches to stopping human rights abuses.

"Amnesty [International] has helped to liberate 25,000 political prisoners."

NONGOVERNMENTAL ORGANIZATIONS EFFECTIVELY COMBAT HUMAN RIGHTS ABUSES

Robert F. Drinan

Nongovernmental human rights organizations such as Amnesty International are effective crusaders for human rights, argues Robert F. Drinan in the following viewpoint. According to Drinan, Amnesty International stops human rights violations by alerting the world to governmental human rights abuses and by organizing successful campaigns to end the torture, mistreatment, and wrongful detainment of political dissidents. Drinan is a law professor at the Georgetown University Law Center in Washington, D.C.

As you read, consider the following questions:

1. According to Drinan, what are the origins of Amnesty International?
2. How did an "urgent action message" help to free a political prisoner in Chile in the 1980s, according to the author?
3. In how many nations were prisoners abused or tortured in 1994, according to Drinan?

Reprinted from Robert F. Drinan, "Report on Amnesty International," Commonweal, October 7, 1994, by permission.

I first became closely acquainted with Amnesty International in November 1976, when I was on an Amnesty delegation to Argentina, a nation which in March 1976 had been taken over by a military coup. Accompanied by Sir Eric Avebury, a member of the British House of Lords, and a staff member from the London office of Amnesty, I helped to conduct inquiries for several days, wrote the report, gave the government thirty days to reply to it, and then released it.

The process was scrupulously fair, comprehensive, and impartial. Although Amnesty International had not yet won the Nobel Peace Prize, the military and government-controlled press in Buenos Aires knew the worldwide power of Amnesty. The visiting human rights delegation was excoriated in the press and Amnesty was scorned as a Communist front. My rejoinder that Amnesty had just recently published a definitive study of the horrors of the Soviet Gulag never made the press in Argentina.

The Impact of Amnesty International

Since 1976 my admiration for Amnesty has increased in every way. The publication of Amnesty's thirty-second annual report confirms and deepens my appreciation and gratitude for this organization established by an English Catholic attorney in 1961 after he became angry when he read of the brutal repression carried out on citizens in Portugal. This man, Peter Benenson, deliberately chose Trinity Sunday in 1961 to launch Amnesty. It was an appropriate year, Mr. Benenson noted, because it commemorated the hundredth anniversary of the emancipation of the slaves in America and the liberation of the serfs in Russia.

Amnesty now has 1.1 million members in over 150 countries. There are 4,349 local units plus several thousand university and other groups in eighty nations. On October 1, 1993, Amnesty was working on 3,507 "action files" involving 8,906 persons and had so far that year initiated 551 urgent appeals to its networks across the globe. These new actions were issued on behalf of people who had been victims of torture, political killings, disappearances, or similar serious violations of human rights.

I personally witnessed the impact of an "urgent action message" from Amnesty. In the 1980s I was on a human rights mission in Chile—immediately before Augusto Pinochet was removed from office by a democratic election. The government in Santiago had just imprisoned and sentenced to interior exile a prominent physician because he had stated openly that the government was engaged in torturing political dissidents. Within a day Amnesty had alerted over fifty nations to launch a protest.

The ambassadors of these nations in Chile brought intense pressure on the Pinochet government to release this political prisoner. Within seventy-two hours the outspoken doctor was back with his family.

A NETWORK OF RESOURCES

A recent visit to Amnesty's London headquarters reminded me of the vast, worldwide network of resources which the organization possesses. I was not prepared for the intense security around Amnesty's building in London, but clearly tyrants everywhere in the world would like to destroy the files kept there.

The 1994 report reveals the details of Amnesty's somber mission. In 112 nations prisoners were tortured or abused. Political assassinations occurred in sixty-one countries. The extent of the human rights violations in countries from Afghanistan to Zimbabwe is appalling. The report also discloses the persistent, pervasive, and penetrating messages Amnesty sent to the world press. The 352-page annual report also describes at some length the intense collaboration which Amnesty International maintains with human rights groups, both public and private, across the globe.

I saw that collaboration at its finest in 1993 during the eight days of the UN World Conference on Human Rights in Vienna. I was there as a representative of the American Bar Association and witnessed the magnificent leadership which Amnesty gave to other nongovernmental organizations and to the entire conference. Amnesty was looked to by everyone as a principal architect of that remarkable gathering, which brought together delegates from 154 nations and from two thousand nongovernmental organizations.

THE CRUSADE FOR HUMAN RIGHTS

Amnesty's crusade for human rights concentrates on political rather than economic rights. Central to its agenda is an opposition to capital punishment. In annual report after annual report the entry about the United States repeats Amnesty's condemnation of the practice, and notes that the death penalty has been abolished everywhere in Europe and in almost every nation in Latin America.

Amnesty is also the world's clearinghouse for information about the progress of the ratification of the United Nations covenant on human rights. Again the United States lags behind almost every other nation. In June 1994, the United States finally ratified the international covenant on political and interna-

The protection of human rights defenders continues to be a high priority for Amnesty International. The focus throughout 1996 was on Latin America, a region with a particularly long tradition of standing up for human rights in dangerous circumstances: over the last decade, hundreds of human rights activists have been assassinated or made to "disappear" for investigating and denouncing state violence and political killings. The repression continued in 1996: defenders were harassed or had their work curtailed through ostensibly legal channels—their writing was banned or censored, official restrictions denied them freedom of movement and the right to organize themselves or prevented them from representing victims. Defenders received death threats, their phones were tapped, their houses were watched, their families were intimidated. Many had to flee their countries.

Amnesty International could not function without the information and assistance provided by these brave men and women, and shares a responsibility with other international and national organizations to protect and support them.

Amnesty International Report, 1997.

---

tional rights, but has yet to ratify major UN covenants on the rights of women and children. Indeed, the United States has not even ratified the American Convention on Human Rights, thus depriving the United States of a voice and vote in the Inter-American Commission and Court of Human Rights based in Costa Rica.

The massive outpouring of literature from Amnesty is filled with facts, names, and tragic stories. There is no concentration on theory or philosophy. Amnesty, in its own words, wants to orchestrate a "mobilization of shame." And it has succeeded far better than could conceivably have been imagined by its founder in 1961.

STANDING FOR HUMAN DIGNITY

When I speak at the first meeting of the Amnesty chapter at Georgetown University Law Center each fall, I usually remind the students that Amnesty has helped to liberate 25,000 political prisoners. I also recall the stirring statement made by Amnesty on the occasion of its twenty-fifth anniversary—a statement which epitomizes the very essence of its mission:

When you do something to help a prisoner of conscience or to try to save someone from torture, you are doing something of incalculable value—even if it may seem very modest to you. You are taking a stand for human dignity. You are saying that you refuse to accept the torture, the humiliation, and the silencing of another human being. In the face of cruelty and the arrogant abuse of limitless power, you are proving—by personal example—to both the victims and their tormentors that compassion, justice, and human love are still alive.

"Expression of outrage against bad prison conditions has been more consistent than outrage at genocide."

NONGOVERNMENTAL ORGANIZATIONS ARE INEFFECTIVE

Alexander Cockburn

Most nongovernmental human rights organizations are ineffective, contends Alexander Cockburn in the following viewpoint. For example, Cockburn points out, the activism of several nongovernmental organizations (NGOs) failed to prevent the genocide of the Tutsis in Rwanda in 1994. Cockburn concludes that combating or acquiring state power is more effective than NGO activism in promoting human rights. Cockburn is a columnist for the *Nation*, a weekly progressive newsjournal.

As you read, consider the following questions:

1. According to Alex de Waal as quoted by the author, what is the difference between "primary movements" and professional human rights organizations?
2. How did some NGOs attempt to avert the genocide in Rwanda, according to Cockburn?
3. According to the author, how has human rights activism in Rwanda unwittingly allowed genocidal criminals to escape punishment?

Reprinted from Alexander Cockburn, "The Decay of 'Human Rights,'" *Liberal Opinion Week*, April 14, 1997, by permission of Alexander Cockburn and Creators Syndicate.

The human-rights movement is in a state of profound crisis, yet human-rights professionals continue blithely on as though nothing untoward had occurred. But something very untoward did occur back in 1994. The Hutu in Rwanda launched the first unquestioned genocide since the Second World War, and although it was covered by the press in horrifying detail, the human-rights community wasn't able to do a thing about it. Years later, the full implications of that failure should surely be sinking in.

THE "HUMAN-RIGHTS" CAREER

Alex de Waal, co-director of London-based Africa Rights, makes a distinction between what he calls "primary movements" and the professional human-rights organizations that came into being in the mid-1970s. The primary movements of an earlier decade—the U.S. civil rights movement and the women's movement, for example—were "mass popular movements dedicated to the struggle for democratic rights," pursuing specific political principles.

By contrast, the 1975 Helsinki Accords, committing Eastern Bloc countries to respect basic human rights, engendered what de Waal calls the archetypal second-generation human-rights organization, Helsinki Watch, put together by publishers, lawyers and some civil-rights veterans. It concentrated on using the media and lobbying politicians; money came from wealthy foundations, such as Ford. The profession of human-rights activism was created, marrying legalism with journalism and political lobbying, shortcutting the erstwhile belief that it was necessary to build a mass political constituency. "Human Rights" became a career: high-profile, risk-free and commanding a professional salary.

The prime strategy of the human-rights pros was, in the words of Aryeh Neier, founder of Human Rights Watch, "mobilizing shame." It's a mobilization that has been yielding diminishing returns, as the jaunts of Al Gore and Newt Gingrich to China have demonstrated. And of course, "human rights" had a lot more resonance in Washington in the years of the Cold War, often successfully corralled in the interests of the state.

INEFFECTIVE ACTIVISM

De Waal points out that between the onset of political liberalization in 1990 and the genocide in 1994, Rwanda had "an exemplary human-rights community." There were no less than seven indigenous human-rights Non-Governmental Organizations (NGOs), with allies and patrons overseas, which reported closely on the mounting waves of massacres and murders. In

January of 1993, these NGOs invited an Internal Commission of Inquiry, which named some of the perpetrators. The NGOs even predicted monstrous atrocities unless something were done to curb and punish these perpetrators. "But," as de Waal says, "there was no primary movement that could underpin the activists' agenda, no political establishment ready to listen to their critique and act on it, and no international organization ready to take the measures and risks necessary to protect them."

Jeff Danziger. Copyright ©1997 The Christian Science Publishing Society. Distributed by the Los Angeles Times Syndicate. Reprinted with permission.

And then, on April 6, 1994, the Hutu began their final solution, butchering the Tutsis and all critics. The United Nations took to its heels. In probably its most shameful act to date, the Clinton administration did nothing, worse than nothing, putting up Secretary of State Warren Christopher and his subordinates to say that "acts of genocide may have been committed and need to be investigated," which meant that the United States was able to evade its obligations as laid down in the 1949 Genocide Convention. The Hutus' only mistake was to encounter defeat by the Rwandese Patriotic Front.

Thus, the first indisputable genocide since that same 1949 Convention aroused no international revulsion powerful enough to compel intervention. This, after almost 20 years of human-rights professional campaigning. "Arguably," de Waal charges, "one reason is the existence of specialist human-rights institutions: responsibility for responding was seen to be theirs, not all of humanity's." Human-rights activism had been routinized, and as de Waal points out, the United Nations and most human-rights NGOs "have devoted more resources to documenting the revenge killings of Tutsi soldiers and shortcomings of the new government than they have spent in investigating the worst crime against humanity to have occurred since their creation and in bringing the killers to justice. Expression of outrage against bad prison conditions has been more consistent than outrage at genocide."

BUSINESS AS USUAL

So we have human rights as "business as usual," in which genocide becomes pigeonholed as "past abuses," and thus minimized, in contrast to "current abuses" about which the human-rights pros can raise their stink. The genocide is gently waved away in the name of "reconciliation," while some human-rights pros suggest that there somehow has been a "double genocide" with blame attaching to both sides. Overall, as de Waal says, the unfortunate reality is that human-rights activism in post-genocide Rwanda has done more to encourage impunity for genocidal criminals than to bring to justice those responsible.

A reinvention of human-rights professionalism is in order. De Waal suggests that "contesting or gaining state power can be the most effective way to advance human rights" and that recognition of this fact means "abandoning the human-rights NGO as the privileged vehicle for achieving human rights." I thought about this remark on April 1, 1997, after seeing a photograph in the newspaper of Laurent Kabila addressing his rebel troops in Kisangani. Back when Kabila was campaigning with Che Guevara in the Congo in the mid-1960s, de Waal's observation about the seizure of state power would have been regarded as self-evident to the point of being trite. Maybe the wheel is turning full circle, though the human-rights professionals will cling limpet-like to their futile strategies and to their sinecures.

| "The 'kinder, gentler' workplace is an achievable first step and many workers will be glad for it."

FACTORIES SHOULD BE REQUIRED TO ADHERE TO MINIMUM STANDARDS

Abigail McCarthy

Many U.S. companies have been criticized for selling goods made in foreign sweatshops—factories in which workers face inhumane treatment. In response to this criticism, a governmental commission consisting of representatives from industries, unions, consumers, religious groups, and human rights organizations has compiled a list of minimum standards that requires these overseas plants to provide humane working conditions. In the following viewpoint, Abigail McCarthy argues in support of these minimum standards. Such standards, she argues, will end child labor, provide safe working environments, and guarantee workers the right to organize. McCarthy is a columnist for *Commonweal*, a biweekly Catholic journal.

As you read, consider the following questions:

1. What happened to Iqbal Masih of Pakistan, according to McCarthy?
2. According to the author, why have some human rights organizations criticized the list of minimum standards for overseas factories?
3. In McCarthy's opinion, why should pressure groups also focus on factories in the United States?

Reprinted from Abigail McCarthy, "Kinder, Gentler Sweatshops," *Commonweal*, June 6, 1997, by permission.

R eaders may remember the valiant twelve-year-old Iqbal Masih of Pakistan whose courageous crusade for the human rights of the child laborers of his country aroused those of us in the first world to the dire situation of millions of children in the third. He awakened us, too, to our unwitting complicity in that situation via America's global industries. He reminded us that our clothes and our shoes are imported far too often from American-owned sweatshops abroad in which children (and adults too) work in shocking conditions.

IQBAL'S STORY

Iqbal was made to work in a carpet factory when he was only four. He worked twelve hours a day, sometimes more, with a half-hour break for lunch. If he was ill or lagged behind, he was beaten or hung upside down. At the age of ten, with unusual spirit, he attended a meeting of the Bonded Labor Liberation Front and learned that his bondage was illegal. He obtained a "certificate of freedom" and began school and his fight to free other children. Iqbal was a martyr for his cause, shot while riding his bicycle—murdered, many think, because he had angered the wealthy and powerful "carpet masters."

In April 1997, as the anniversary of Iqbal's death approached, Kamran Aslam Khan, minister of trade at the Embassy of Pakistan, in Washington, D.C., issued a letter marking the occasion "with profound grief and sorrow." Iqbal's contribution, Mr. Khan wrote, "in raising the general consciousness of human-rights issues and more specifically issues pertaining to the exploitation of children," has resulted in remedial initiatives the world over and, of course, in Pakistan.

RECOGNIZING THE PROBLEM OF CHILD LABOR

Somewhat defensively, the minister reports on two surveys done in collaboration with the International Labor Organization that "have confirmed our conviction that the incidence of child labor in Pakistan is not of alarming proportions" and that "the figures quoted in the international media were absolutely incor-- rect." True, there are 3.5 million children employed in the country, but only 11 percent are in the manufacturing and transport sectors (the object of Iqbal's concern). The great majority—70 percent—are employed in "the informal sector . . . including family business, domestic service, home-based industries, shops, and small establishments." Another 19 percent are working in crafts and their sales.

But "whatever its magnitude," the minister concludes, "the

government . . . is cognizant of the child-labor problem and is committed to combat it through programs designated to implement laws, coupled with measures to rehabilitate the . . . children after withdrawal from their place of work." (Skeptics should remember that Iqbal won his freedom through the Bonded Labor Liberation Front, which had its source in the Bonded Labor System [Abolition] Act passed in 1992, and that he attended a BLLF school.) The other initiatives in Pakistan, listed by the minister, are impressive.

PROMOTING HUMANE WORKING CONDITIONS

Whether by coincidence or design, Mr. Khan's report was issued at about the same time as a White House report on an agreement of several U.S. companies—including Nike and Liz Claiborne—to promulgate a set of minimum standards for their overseas plants and subcontractors. The agreement had its roots in a meeting in August 1996 when President Bill Clinton and then-Secretary of Labor Robert Reich called together representatives of the apparel and shoe industries, trade unions, a consumer federation, and religious and human-rights organizations. They were asked to prepare a plan to promote humane working conditions here and overseas. It was also an acknowledgment of the fact that sweatshops overseas are beyond the reach of U.S. law but not beyond the influence of U.S. companies with factories abroad.

A GOOD START

Will the "No Sweat" labels, so coveted by the [apparel-industry] companies, be meaningful guides for consumers when they are finally awarded, or will they become mere public relations devices that serve to obscure rather than eliminate workplace abuses?

The latter could happen in the absence of real safeguards. But at some point on difficult issues you have to take a chance. You have to move. If the companies act in good faith on just the issues that have already been agreed upon, many workers around the world will be helped.

Bob Herbert, New York Times, April 14, 1997.

In addition to the agreement of companies to issue standards, the participants agreed that the commission as a whole was to become a nonprofit foundation monitoring compliance. And the commission was to enlist companies not part of the first gathering, as well as other companies beyond the manufacturers of apparel and shoes. The pledged standards, though termed minimum, were significant: to end child labor and forced labor; to provide a safe and healthy working environment; to guarantee the rights to organize and to collective bargaining.

A CONSTRUCTIVE BEGINNING

Almost at once, some human-rights groups were up in arms. They said, among other things, that the commission had only succeeded in getting "a kinder, gentler sweat shop." Why accept, for example, the legal minimum wage of various countries—which falls far short of meeting workers' needs (seventy cents, for example)—instead of imposing a living minimum wage? Was it not outrageous to tolerate sixty-hour workweeks with only one day off? And why not demand complete independence for those who monitor working conditions?

Unfortunately, the "kinder, gentler" workplace is an achievable first step and many workers will be glad for it. It is a constructive beginning. Only continued public pressure on this issue will make the commission succeed. It behooves all people of conscience to contribute to that pressure. Some companies have complied not so much out of good will but because of bad publicity. Even at the time of the report, Indonesian police were battling Nike workers who were demonstrating because they purportedly were not being paid the legal $2.50 minimum wage. And in Vietnam it was reported that young women making Nike sneakers were earning less per day than the cost of an adequate diet.

Pressure against sweatshops and the concomitant abuse of human rights is, alas, needed in the United States too. Here the pressure must focus on the uncovering of sweatshops and the enforcement of the existing laws. How soon we have forgotten the discovery of the factory on the West Coast and the enslavement of Thai women immigrants there.

Representative George Miller (D-Calif.) has recently introduced legislation to impose federal minimum-wage and immigration laws on the Commonwealth of the Northern Mariana Islands (CNMI), a U.S. territory. The government there, he said, has allowed sweatshop conditions, forced prostitution, and the exploitation of foreign workers. Noting the recently announced agreement of the U.S. manufacturers and the administration in regard to sweatshops overseas, he said, "Those efforts must also focus on our own soil, on the CNMI, where conditions that could not be tolerated anywhere else in America flourish with the blessings of the local government."

"We cannot leave the fate of the
world's apparel workers in the hands
of presidential commissions."

MINIMUM FACTORY STANDARDS
WILL NOT PREVENT HUMAN
RIGHTS ABUSES

Medea Benjamin

Many U.S. companies that have factories in foreign countries
have agreed to adopt the minimum standards for treatment of
factory workers that were drawn up by a coalition of industry,
labor, and human rights groups. In the following viewpoint,
Medea Benjamin contends that these minimum standards are
not enough to protect workers' human rights. According to Benjamin, these standards will not guarantee workers a living wage,
freedom from mandatory overtime, or the right to collective
bargaining. Benjamin is the director of Global Exchange, a San
Francisco–based human rights organization.

As you read, consider the following questions:

1. What are the wages of Nike workers in Vietnam, according to
   Benjamin?
2. How could a U.S. company truly guarantee the rights of its
   foreign workers to organize, in the author's opinion?
3. In Benjamin's opinion, who should monitor the working
   conditions of foreign factories?

Reprinted from Medea Benjamin, "No Sweat for Companies to Agree," Los Angeles Times,
April 17, 1997, by permission of the author.

With much fanfare at a Rose Garden ceremony, President Clinton announced that a coalition of industry, human rights and labor groups had reached a breakthrough agreement to end sweatshops. Saying that the lives of factory workers are as important as the fabric they make, President Clinton called the agreement a historic step that will "give American consumers greater confidence in the products they buy." Companies that voluntarily adhere to this new code will be able to tag their products "sweatshop free."

But before consumers go on a guilt-free shopping spree, they should take a moment to look at some of the details of this agreement.

A Breakthrough Agreement?

• *Companies shall pay the prevailing minimum wage or industry wage.* Companies are flocking to countries that deliberately set the minimum wage below subsistence to attract foreign investment. In Vietnam, Nike pays 20 cents an hour; in Haiti, Disney pays 30 cents an hour. These wages, while the legal minimum, are not enough to buy three decent meals a day, let alone pay for transportation, housing, clothing and health care. U.S. companies should pay wages that allow workers to live healthy, dignified lives. They should swiftly and publicly commit themselves to paying at least double the legal minimum in their overseas factories. And they should agree to pay restitution to workers who have been cheated out of past wages.

• *Except in extraordinary business circumstances, employees shall not be required to work more than 60 hours a week.* In addition to accepting a 60-hour week as the norm—which in itself is outrageous—the agreement provides no guidelines on what constitutes "extraordinary circumstances." Moreover, it only addresses "mandatory" overtime. Already, apparel factory workers put in endless "voluntary" overtime. There should be no mandatory overtime and if workers were paid a living wage for an eight-hour day, excessive "voluntary" overtime would cease.

• *Employees shall be compensated for overtime hours at the legal rate, or where none exists, at a rate at least equal to their regular hourly compensation rate.* Labor unions the world over call for overtime to be paid at a higher rate than the regular hourly wage. The agreement should call for at least time-and-a-half pay for overtime.

• *Employers shall recognize and respect the right of employees to freedom of association and collective bargaining.* Recognition of these rights is certainly a positive step. Unfortunately, many U.S. companies choose to work in countries or free-trade zones where independent organizing is illegal and where workers who stand up for their rights are severely repressed. To give this recognition of workers' rights meaning, U.S. companies must pressure local governments to allow workers the freedom to organize, call for the release of all those jailed for their organizing efforts and require companies to rehire in their own factories workers who have been fired for organizing.

Reprinted by permission of Clay Bennett, North America Syndicate.

• *Companies shall utilize independent external monitors to ensure that the [agreement] is implemented.* The agreement does not insist that companies use local human rights, labor or religious groups that have the trust of the workers and knowledge of local conditions. Instead, the companies can use private accounting firms and merely "consult regularly" with these local institutions. It is extremely unlikely that employees working under repressive conditions would speak openly to representatives of accounting firms. Meaningful monitoring must be conducted by respected not-for-profit entities.

More Action Is Needed

According to this agreement, companies could still pay their workers 20 cents an hour, coerce them into countless hours of "voluntary overtime," use accounting firms that have no connection to workers as their external monitors and be rewarded for this behavior with a "no sweatshop" seal of approval.

The results of this task force's eight-month process demonstrate all too clearly that we cannot leave the fate of the world's apparel workers in the hands of presidential commissions. To really put an end to sweatshops, we must continue to mobilize public opinion, support struggling factory workers and pressure abusive corporations until workers at home and abroad are paid living wages and treated with dignity.

"By granting asylum to women . . .
the United States could send a
powerful message to those who
distort religion to justify terror."

PERSECUTED WOMEN SHOULD BE GIVEN POLITICAL ASYLUM

Part I: Katha Pollitt, Part II: Geraldine Brooks

In the following two-part viewpoint, Katha Pollitt and Geraldine Brooks contend that women subjected to persecution in their home countries should be granted political asylum in the United States. In Part I, Pollitt maintains that women fleeing the practice of female genital mutilation deserve support and refuge in the United States. In Part II, Brooks argues that asylee status should be given to victims of antifemale religious persecution in male-dominated societies. Pollitt is an associate editor for the *Nation*, a progressive journal of opinion. Brooks is the author of *Nine Points of Desire: The Hidden World of Islamic Women*.

As you read, consider the following questions:

1. In what ways has the U.S. government's human rights policy been inconsistent, in Pollitt's opinion?
2. According to Pollitt, how could avoiding a stance on female genital mutilation be a form of cultural imperialism?
3. Why did Naima Belahi seek political asylum in the United States, according to Brooks?

Part I is reprinted from Katha Pollitt, "Women's Rights, Human Rights," *Nation*, May 13, 1997, by permission of the *Nation* magazine. Part II is reprinted from Geraldine Brooks, "Asylum Policy Shortchanges Women," *San Diego Union-Tribune*, March 12, 1995 (originally appearing as an editorial in the *New York Times*), by permission of the author.

Are women's rights human rights? During the cold war the United States granted political refugee status to virtually any escapee from the Soviet Union and its satellites, a policy that persisted, with regard to Cuba, until recently. Yet even by the narrowest definition of political rights, millions of women around the globe are as deprived as were the inhabitants of the evil empire—unable to vote, travel freely, own property, speak their minds. By any more expansive definition of liberty, even more millions of women qualify as human rights victims. For all its faults, Communism did not permit the legal murder of women by male relatives for supposed crimes against the family "honor," use rape as a weapon of terror, deny widows custody of their children or permit young girls to be sold into polygynous marriages.

INCONSISTENT HUMAN RIGHTS POLICIES

That's not the way our government sees it, of course: Can you imagine Jimmy Carter inviting, say, Pakistan to release to the U.S. its rape victims jailed for the crime of fornication in the same buoyant spirit he dared Castro to let loose the Marielitos [125,000 Cubans released in 1980 who reached the United States by boat]? If one took seriously the government's fine words on human rights, one could not begin to understand how George Bush declared the one-child policy of China a human rights violation justifying American asylum for any Chinese affected by it while ignoring the four-child policy of Ceausescu's Romania, which featured many of the same totalitarian measures—mandatory gynecological inspections, coercive monitoring of pregnancies, economic sanctions for reproductive noncooperators. Still less could one understand how we came to defend Kuwait, of all places, as a bastion of democracy, producing the truly weird paradox of U.S. women soldiers flexing their newly won military muscles to reinstate a barely constitutional monarchy that denied most men and all women the vote and in which all the real work seems to have been performed by Palestinian engineers and Asian housemaids.

Given the government's flexible and convenient notions of human rights—Cuba si, Haiti non; Libya bad, Saudi Arabia good—it's not surprising that the Immigration and Naturalization Service (I.N.S.) resisted offering a refuge from female genital mutilation [F.G.M.] to 19-year-old Fauziya Kasinga of Togo, despite its own guidelines defining F.G.M. as a form of persecution, and kept her in prison for almost two years, also despite its own rules. What is significant, though, is that her case has become a cause célèbre, with support from Equality Now—an international feminist organization that has long struggled against F.G.M.—the Center for Reproductive Law and Policy, Amnesty International and other human rights groups. In a day of conversations with feminists and human rights activists, I only once heard the argument, so common ten or even five years ago, that F.G.M. is a time-honored "cultural practice," opposition to which is a form of Western cultural imperialism.

VIOLATIONS OF WOMEN'S HUMAN RIGHTS

Female genital mutilation (FGM) is an ever growing practice of horror and torture that has hurt an estimated 130 million women and girls world wide. It is estimated that by the year 2000 approximately 220 million girls will suffer this mutilation. . . .

Feminists dislike using the term "female circumcision" because it minimizes and implies a fallacious analogy to non-mutilating male circumcision, it which skin is cut without damaging the organ. The male equivalent of "female circumcision" or "clitoridectomy" (another common term for this procedure) would be the amputation of most of the penis, a "penisectomy."

FGM is a practice of culture, not religion. It was spread by dominant tribes and civilizations. It is the ultimate example of the subjugation of women.

The burning of Indian widows, the binding of the female Chinese feet, the sale of Taiwanese children into sexual slavery are and were preserved under centuries of tradition. All are extreme examples of violations of the human rights of women, as is female genital mutilation.

Lynn M. Tynan, *Off Our Backs*, June 1997.

This seems to me a major shift. Until quite recently, F.G.M. tended to be ignored or minimized by those with an interest in the developing world, including leftists and feminists. It was euphemized as "female circumcision," although the operation—in which the clitoris, the labia and sometimes the entire vulva are sliced off and the vaginal opening sewn up—is a medically disastrous, sometimes even fatal, procedure with grave consequences: excruciating pain, recurring infections, the destruction of sexual pleasure and lifelong difficulties with urination, menstruation, intercourse and childbirth. Germaine Greer mentions it only once in *Sex and Destiny*, her hymn to what she imagines is traditional Third World family life. Like many of F.G.M.'s apologists, she portrays it as a folkway of a few African tribes, when it is in fact practiced in more than 25 countries in Africa—Egypt, Sudan, Somalia, Ethiopia, Kenya, Nigeria—and is found as well in the Middle East and Asia, producing an estimated 100 million victims in all. A few years ago, when I briefly mentioned F.G.M. in the same breath as foot-binding in [an editorial in the Nation], I received letters castigating me for failing to equate it with such American beauty practices as breast implants and high heels. Breast implants are performed on consenting adults, though, not children—and a woman can always take off her Kenneth Coles.

THE REAL CULTURAL IMPERIALISM

Actually, one could argue that failing to take a stand against F.G.M. is the real cultural imperialism. The U.N. and UNICEF are on record against it, and all the countries in which it is practiced have indigenous groups and individuals working to eradicate it—just as there are plenty of Irish women who fight their country's abortion ban and American women who fight for the rights of battered women. No more than the industrialized West is Egypt or Nigeria a static society in which "tradition" rules unchallenged. One of the interesting, tragic things about Stephanie Welsh's photos of a Kenyan F.G.M. ritual, which won the 1996 Pulitzer Prize in photography, is that the girl pictured was the first and only one in her village to go to high school. Fauziya Kasinga's father opposed F.G.M. and polygyny and was able to protect his four older daughters from both; it was his sudden death that put Fauziya, then 17, into the hands of an aunt with other ideas. So the question for Westerners is really, Whom do you support? Fauziya and her sisters, or the aunt and the 45-year-old man whose fourth wife Fauziya was forced to become?

There are difficult and delicate questions about how Westerners can best help indigenous groups fight F.G.M. in their own countries. Many people I spoke with, indeed, argued that insensitive Western involvement had backfired, causing people to cling to the practice as a form of cultural resistance. Surely, though, Americans can hold our own government to the human rights standards it professes. By those standards, Fauziya Kasinga and other women who flee F.G.M. are heroines who deserve the warmest of welcomes.

II

She makes women's clothes. In today's Algeria, that is a political act, and potentially a fatal one.

Until 1994, when she abandoned her market stall in Algiers, 38-year-old Naima Belahi imported fabric from France and Italy and sewed it into beaded evening gowns or stylish short dresses.

Then, on March 10, 1994, Algeria's Islamic insurgents ordered all women to veil themselves within a week or risk becoming targets of murder. The day after the deadline, militants killed a 16-year-old high school student who was walking to class without a head scarf.

Belahi, visiting the United States at the time, was afraid to return home. She neither makes nor wears the shroudlike Islamic dress that must cover the female body. To do so, she feels, would be to signal agreement with the extremists.

She has taken refuge with a Connecticut family and applied for political asylum.

SHORTCHANGING PERSECUTED WOMEN

Unfortunately for Belahi, her case has fallen into a chaotic system that almost never considers persecution of women a basis for asylum.

Despite growing worldwide abuse of women by religious extremists—not just in Algeria but also in Afghanistan, Sudan, the Gaza Strip and Saudi Arabia—the Immigration and Naturalization Service works from a sketchy manual that advises against accepting most sex-based claims.

Asylum seekers must show a "well-founded fear of persecution."

This can be based on race, religion, nationality or political views. Less commonly, it can be based on membership in a "particular social group" that is subject to abuse.

In Algeria, more than 50 women have been killed since the Islamic insurgency began in 1992. Many more have been knifed or raped for working alongside men or wearing Western dress.

The murdered women have included the principal of a co-ed school, a secretary who worked at a police station to support her unemployed siblings, and a 22-year-old woman wearing jeans and buying cigarettes—enough to identify her to the militants as a "prostitute."

CULTURAL MORES OR ABUSE?

Yet when an Algerian doctor applied for asylum here in 1995, saying she had been threatened with death because she supervised male physicians, the INS case officer said that violence in Algeria was "too random" to support her claim to belong to a "particular social group" at risk of persecution.

If Algeria's violence is considered too random to warrant asylum, awkward questions arise about countries—including a close U.S. ally, Saudi Arabia—where abuse of women is systemic. In 1993, after almost two years of deliberation, Canada granted asylum to a Saudi student known as Nada who had argued that she risked flogging and imprisonment for walking in the street with her hair and face uncovered.

In the United States, asylum experts say that Nada's predicament would most likely have been viewed by the INS as a matter of cultural mores rather than as persecution.

But substitute race for sex and the American position seems untenable.

Imagine a country half black and half white, where the blacks may not legally leave the house without a white's permission, or where they may be caned in the street for refusing to wear the official segregating dress. That is the situation for women in Saudi Arabia.

SENDING A MESSAGE
In the spring of 1994, some experts in immigration law at Harvard Law School submitted guidelines on asylum for women to the INS with the hope that they might become the basis for a fairer assessment of claims of persecution.

With anti-immigrant sentiment rampant in the Republican Congress, however, any attempt to liberalize INS standards is sure to meet resistance.

Yet asylum seekers constitute a tiny fraction of the people seeking admission to the United States each year. Opening the gate wider to persecuted women is hardly likely to result in a flood of new applicants. Most of the persecuted women live in countries where men control their right to leave the country, or even the house.

By granting asylum to women such as Belahi, the Algerian seamstress, the United States could send a powerful message to those who distort religion to justify terror.

The message would be that Americans, too, hold certain things sacred—and among them are liberty, equality, the pursuit of happiness and the right to hold one's own beliefs.

"Expressed opposition to female circumcision . . . does not meet internationally recognized grounds for seeking asylum in the U.S."

POLITICAL ASYLUM SHOULD NOT BE GIVEN TO ALL WOMEN CLAIMING PERSECUTION

Wayne Lutton

Women who claim they are fleeing persecution in their home country should not always be given political asylum in the United States, argues Wayne Lutton in the following viewpoint. According to Lutton, asylum status should not be granted to women suffering from domestic abuse or women who disagree with their home culture's traditions because then millions of potential asylees could flood the borders of the United States. These numbers would strain the ability of the United States to control immigration levels and manage its population, Lutton claims. Furthermore, he maintains, since no governments force women to undergo female circumcision, claiming to be a potential victim of the practice should not be considered grounds for asylum. Lutton is coauthor of The Immigration Invasion and the associate editor of the Social Contract, a quarterly journal that examines the issues of immigration and population growth.

As you read, consider the following questions:

1. What is the difference between a refugee and an asylee, according to Lutton?
2. According to the author, what percentage of asylum applicants permanently remain in the United States?
3. What steps could governments take to oppose the practice of female genital mutilation, according to Lutton?

Reprinted from Wayne Lutton, "Fleeing Their Culture: Extending Asylum to Women," Social Contract, Summer 1997, by permission.

The United States has, from time to time and in select cases, provided a safe haven for individuals genuinely subject to persecution by the government of their homeland. But not all fleeing oppression in foreign lands have been made welcome. Refugee admissions did not really become a public policy concern until the World War II era and the subsequent onset of the Cold War. Such refugees and Displaced Persons who were admitted arrived under special legislation aimed at addressing special circumstances. There was no intention of permitting any and all who might wish to come to the United States to do so.

A popular misperception is that the U.S. has a long "tradition" of admitting endless streams of refugees. In fact, it was not until 1980 that Congress enacted a specific Refugee Act. This law accepted the United Nations Organization definition of a refugee, namely: a person living outside of their homeland who is unable or unwilling to return to that country because of a well-grounded fear of government-sponsored persecution due to the individual's race, religion, nationality, membership in a particular social group, or political opinions.

REFUGEES AND ASYLEES

For the sake of law, definitions are important. Refugees are persons living outside of the U.S. who have a "well-founded fear of persecution" and who apply for refugee status. Asylees are persons already in the U.S., or who have just arrived at a port of entry, who claim that they will be subjected to persecution and oppression should they be forced to return home. They apply for asylum.

The drafters of the 1980 Refugee Act asserted that the intake of refugees and asylum seekers be less than 5,000 per year. But the Refugee Act failed to include a cap or ceiling on annual admissions. In practice, the number of refugees and asylees admitted every year since the 1980 Act took effect has never been under 50,000. Since 1989, yearly admissions have averaged nearly 120,000.

This still understates the number of people admitted under our asylum laws. For FY [Fiscal Year] 1995, for example, refugee admissions were set at 112,000. However, there is currently no limit on the number of people who may apply for asylum in any given year. In FY 1995, 149,566 foreigners filed asylum applications. During the first six months of FY 1996, there were an additional 90,700 applications for asylum.

Most asylum applications are rejected—the approval rate averaged 10 percent before 1993 and has risen to 20 percent under the Clinton Administration. Nonetheless, the INS [Immigration and Naturalization Service] estimates that roughly 80 percent of asylum applicants will remain in the U.S. permanently. No matter how a particular individual's case is resolved, it is the rare person who is forced to leave.

THE EXPANSION OF REFUGEE STATUS

With the end of the Cold War, many expected that the number of people applying for refuge in the U.S. would steadily decline. However, special interests have managed to manipulate refugee policy to favor particular ethnic and social groups. Few of the persons now admitted as refugees meet the UN standard.

Political asylum has recently been extended to include people claiming to be opposed to the community standards and traditions of their native lands. In part, this expansion of "refugee" status mirrors domestic American politics and reflects a desire by Congress and the Executive Branch to curry favor with particular constituents. The original intent of the refugee legislation to offer temporary protection to people who are being persecuted as individuals by their home government has been largely overlooked.

Feminists and other pro-immigration activists have succeeded in expanding the limits of asylum to include suffering from domestic abuse, publicly advocating feminism, or disagreeing with traditions and customs not favored in Western countries. In 1995, Attorney General Janet Reno issued new asylum guidelines that were drafted by the Women Refugee Project at Harvard University.

The guidelines outline examples of social customs and traditions that harm women, such as arranged marriage, slavery, and circumcision, now often referred to as female genital mutilation (FGM). Even expressing opposition to wearing a veil can now be grounds for asylum. Michele Beasley, a member of the Women's Commission for Refugee Women and Children, which advised the Justice Department on this issue, pointed out, "This is a major shift in both the commitment of the agency and in its understanding of the way that the asylum claims of refugee women differ from those of men."

BATTERED WOMEN AS ASYLEES?

In March 1996, the Justice Department issued further guidelines, extending asylum and naturalization opportunities to battered women and children. The so-called "battered spouse waiver" was included in the Violence Against Women Act, a little-noticed provision of the 1994 Crime Bill. The new guidelines amplify how this is to be implemented. According to the new standards, mental as well as physical abuse can be accepted as grounds for asylum in the U.S.

To allay public concerns, INS press releases predicted that only a limited number of "battered spouse" asylum claims were likely to be filed. However, Leslye Orloff, founder of the domestic violence program at Ayuda, a Washington, D.C.-based Hispanic advocacy group, told the *Washington Post* that there might be an initial surge of thousands of such cases nationwide. Alakananda Paul, head of the Asian Women's Self Help Association, went on to note that "physical and mental abuse is common" among the women she works with from such South Asian countries as India, Pakistan, Bangladesh, and Sri Lanka.

A World Bank Study released in June 1997 reported widespread violence against women in the Caribbean and throughout Latin America. Between 25 percent and 50 percent of women south of the border told development agencies they have been abused by male partners. In Mexico, some type of abuse had been committed against women in 70 percent of the homes surveyed. The number of potential asylum applicants from this region alone is in the *tens of millions!*

FEMALE CIRCUMCISION

Many natives of the Third World honor cultural rites that Westerners find revolting. One of these is female circumcision, a custom begun in the 5th century B.C. that is observed by Muslims, Christians, Animists, and adherents of other primitive cults and mystery religions in over 26 countries in Africa, the Middle East, and Asia.

Female genital mutilation take three forms, ranging from a minor ritual cutting or removal of the foreskin of the clitoris, called *Sunna*; excision of the entire clitoris and (usually) the labia minor; to its most extreme form, infibulation (pharaonic circumcision), involving the removal of the clitoris and the labia minora and labia majora, and the joining of the vulva with stitching, leaving only a small opening for urine and menstrual flow. The opening is widened on marriage and for childbirth, but is often resutured after the mother gives birth. There are no sound medical reasons to support any of these procedures.

However disgusting people in the West find FGM, it must be underscored that *no government anywhere forces women to undergo the operation.* Nor do any governments punish females who refuse to comply with this tribal rite. Expressed opposition to female circumcision thus does not meet internationally recognized grounds for seeking asylum in the U.S.

This has not discouraged the Clinton Administration and the Board of Immigration Appeals (BIA) from declaring opposition to FGM good cause for extension of asylum. . . .

THE CASE OF FAUZIYA KASINGA

In one case, decided June 13, 1996, the Board of Immigration Appeals ruled that the practice of female circumcision is a form of "persecution" within the meaning of asylum law. All of the immigration judges who hear asylum cases around the country are currently bound by the BIA's decision.

In this instance, Fauziya Kasinga, a 19-year-old citizen of Togo, applied for asylum after being arrested trying to illegally enter the U.S. with a forged British passport. She asserted that her relatives had arranged a marriage for her with a man in his 40s and that her tribe, the Tchamba-Kunsuntus, practice female circumcision. By her own admission, when she was 17 years of age, Ms. Kasinga left Togo for Ghana, where she failed to file an asylum claim. From Ghana she went on to Germany, where she worked for a while. Once again, she did not appeal for asylum. Instead, she finally made contact with a ring of international alien smugglers, purchased one of their fraudulent British passports, and then attempted to gain entry through Newark International Airport.

THE NEED TO RETHINK REFUGEE POLICY

Our national enthusiasm for welcoming refugees springs from humanitarian and generous motives, and at first glance it would seem above reproach. However, like many other well-intentioned activities, it has side effects. Refugee movement is a significant part of migration to the United States, and immigration levels, along with fertility, largely dictate the rate of growth of the U.S. population. Anybody concerned about unemployment and the fate of the poor, or about our long term ecological future, would do well to learn more about refugee policy, the pressures under which it operates, and the impact it has on immigration and population growth.

Lindsey Grant, NPG Forum, February 1992.

An immigration judge in Baltimore rejected her asylum claim, concluding that her account was "not credible." She appealed. Aided by what USA Today described as an "army of human-rights lawyers," Kasinga and her supporters aimed to establish "a broad policy that any woman or girl who has undergone mutilation in the past or fears it in the future could get asylum."

James H. Walsh, Associate General Counsel of the INS, told the *Washington Post* that the decision to let her stay "is contrary to asylum law." Ms. Kasinga was not subject to persecution by the Togo government. Instead, said Mr. Walsh,

> her travel route is the standard one for economic migrants entering the United States illegally by any means available, who claim asylum only on apprehension. . . . Although female circumcision may well be a centuries-old expression of male domination, it is not a form of government-sponsored persecution required for asylum. In fact, if the young woman from Togo had claimed that her government was denying her the rite, she would have had a stronger asylum case.

EMPTY POLITICAL POSTURING

In the United States, Britain, France, Germany, Italy, the Netherlands, and other Western countries, Third World immigrants are practicing FGM. The states of Minnesota, North Dakota, and California, outlawed FGM, before the U.S. Congress acted in 1996 to impose fines and up to five years imprisonment for individuals found guilty of performing the procedure on girls under the age of 18. Congress also ordered the Department of Health and Human Services to "identify communities in the United States that practice female genital mutilation, and design and carry out outreach activities to educate individuals in the communities on the physical and psychological health effects of such practice."

Further, Congress instructed the Secretary of the Treasury to oppose any loan or other utilization of funds of international financial institutions, other than for basic human needs, for the government of any country which practices FGM and has no educational program in place to prevent its practice. As previously noted, no government in the world currently sponsors FGM. Thus, Public Law 104–208 is another instance of empty political posturing by the U.S. Congress. The action does nothing substantially to reduce the incidence of FGM in the Third World. It is a prime example of what Jeffrey Rosen labels the "age when the president and Congress have marginalized themselves by embracing the politics of symbolic legislation."

CULTURAL RIGHTS

Despite protests from the U.S. Congress, the American Medical Association, the World Health Organization, and a host of international human rights and feminist organizations, Third World nationals are insisting on their right to continue the practice. It is considered "insensitive," "Eurocentric," and "racist" to suggest that such barbaric customs be banned.

Female circumcision has been performed on anywhere from 85 to 114 million women, according to the World Health Organization. Each year, an additional two million girls undergo this primitive rite. And efforts are being made to maintain the practice. In Egypt, which is second only to Israel on the list of U.S. Foreign Aid recipients, a high court recently repealed the Health Ministry's ban on FGM. Sheik Youssef el-Badri, who took Health Minister Ibrahim Sallam to court in 1996, beamed after the verdict: "I will prostrate myself before Allah, thanking him for inspiring the court to take this decision. This is a return to Islam."

Clearly, international human rights organizations face a daunting task in trying to overcome centuries-old customs and belief systems. Perhaps the U.S. and other Western governments could take more active steps to discourage this practice, such as imposing economic sanctions and trade boycotts on countries where FGM continues. No one is yet suggesting that the Third World again come under outside political administration, even though this is likely the only way to outlaw practices Westerners find offensive.

In the wake of the Kasinga decision, immigration lawyers are receiving asylum applications from men, claiming that their wives, daughters, fiancées, and nieces may be subject to female circumcision and that they should thus be allowed to come to the U.S. with them. To how many of these people will we grant asylum?

Refugees Must Be Carefully Screened

The recent expansion of "asylum" to include "culture refugees" qualifies just about everyone living outside the Western World for admission to the U.S. Consequently, current refugee policy opens a door reserved, almost exclusively, for immigrants from the Third World. This corruption of asylum policy must be ended. The distinction between "refugee" and "asylee" is being deliberately blurred. As the noted professor of human ecology, Garrett Hardin, has observed, "the asserted need of people bred in another culture does not confer on them the right to be supported in ours."

Ultimately, the U.S. must reaffirm that it is a Western country and take appropriate measures to secure the best interests of the American majority. Non- and anti-Western people—and the cultures they bring with them—should not be permitted to settle in the United States.

Paradoxically, those who seek refuge elsewhere are most often the very people who best understand the politics, economics, and culture of their homelands and are among the best qualified to help solve problems. They ought to be encouraged to work in their own homelands for desired change.

In the future, admission of any person as a refugee should be done so on an individual basis only after careful screening and on a strictly temporary basis. And refugees should be counted against an overall annual immigration ceiling.

| "The threat of using trade restrictions to advance human rights [in China] is fraught with danger."

FREE TRADE PROMOTES HUMAN RIGHTS IN CHINA

James A. Dorn

The international community has often criticized the Chinese government for its use of prison labor and suppression of political dissidents and religious minorities. Some human rights advocates in the United States have suggested restricting trade with China to pressure its government to abide by internationally accepted human rights standards. James A. Dorn disagrees with this suggestion in the following viewpoint. According to Dorn, economic sanctions would weaken individual autonomy and possibly strengthen Chinese leaders' resolve against political freedom. In Dorn's opinion, free trade should be considered a human right because it fosters tolerance, individual responsibility, and democracy. Dorn is vice president for academic affairs at the Cato Institute, a libertarian research foundation in Washington, D.C.

As you read, consider the following questions:

1. What is the proper duty of government, in Dorn's opinion?
2. According to the author, what is the primary cause of China's lack of respect for human rights?
3. Why would placing high tariffs on Chinese imports be ineffective as an economic sanction, according to Dorn?

Reprinted from James A. Dorn, "Trade and Human Rights: The Case of China," *Cato Journal*, Spring/Summer 1996, by permission of the author.

The rise of democracy in South Korea and Taiwan attests to the power of the market in generating political liberalization. Both countries have moved from closed, authoritarian regimes to open-market democracies without bloody revolutions and without the threat of economic sanctions. The question is, will China follow?

China has created a vibrant economic space by discarding central planning and allowing experimentation with new ownership forms. Since 1979 China's economy has grown at an average annual rate of more than 9 percent and has the potential to become the world's largest economy during the 21st century. Although the Chinese Communist Party (CCP) has held onto its monopoly of political power, China is a more open society today than it was a decade or two ago. There are still serious violations of human rights, but a case can be made that China is creeping along in the right direction and, in time, may follow Taiwan's "quiet revolution."

CHINA AND HUMAN RIGHTS

The critics of China's human rights record are justified in pointing out the abuses that are occurring in China. Yet, many of those critics (e.g., Rep. Nancy Pelosi [D-CA]) underestimate the importance of trade liberalization as a strategy for bringing about systemic change in China. They also fail to distinguish between those human rights that can be universalized and are consistent with individual freedom and those alleged rights that cannot be extended to everyone without violating fundamental rights to life, liberty, and property.

Article 25 of the U.N. Declaration of Human Rights states that each person "has the right to a standard of living adequate for the health and well-being of himself and of his family, including food, clothing, housing and medical care and necessary social services." If sanctions were imposed on China for failing to protect those alleged economic and social "human rights"—rights that cannot be found in the U.S. Bill of Rights, that cannot be universalized, and that cannot be implemented in a world of scarcity—China would become less free and less prosperous. Before acting too hastily, human rights advocates need to think more clearly about the nature of human rights and how best to help China along the path toward a free society.

The threat of using trade restrictions to advance human rights is fraught with danger. Free trade is itself a human right and rests on an individual's rights to life, liberty, and property—rights the U.S. Founding Fathers regarded as inalienable and self-evident. When the federal government closes U.S. markets to countries with governments that deny their citizens certain civil liberties, it robs those citizens of one more freedom and undermines the market dynamic that in the end is the best instrument for creating wealth and preserving freedom.

China serves as a case in point. Denying China most-favored-nation status or imposing sanctions would politicize trade, strengthen the CCP, and harm many innocent people. Sanctions also would violate Americans' rights to liberty and property by interfering with free trade.

FREE TRADE AS A HUMAN RIGHT

The proper function of government is to cultivate a framework for freedom by protecting liberty and property, including freedom of contract (which includes free international trade), not to use the power of government to undermine one freedom in an attempt to secure others. The right to trade is an inherent part of our property rights and a civil right that should be protected as a fundamental human right.

The supposed dichotomy between the right to trade and human rights is a false one. Market exchange rests on private property, which is a natural right. As moral agents, individuals necessarily claim the right to liberty and property in order to live fully and to pursue their interests in a responsible manner. Without private property and freedom of contract, other rights—such as free speech and religious freedom—would have little meaning, because individuals would be at the mercy of the state. The human-rights fabric is not made stronger by unraveling economic liberties in the hope of enhancing other liberties.

Protectionism violates human rights. It is an act of plunder that deprives individuals of their autonomy—an autonomy that precedes any government and is the primary function of just governments to protect. The danger of buying into the argument that restricting trade with China will increase human rights is that such an argument diminishes the significance of the moral case for free trade, politicizes economic life, and weakens the market-liberal vision—a vision that needs to be strengthened in order to protect civil society and human liberty.

THE LOGIC OF TRADE LIBERALIZATION

Those who argue that sanctions will damage a target country's economy enough to bring about political liberalization argue more from emotion than from reason. There is no logical connection between sanctions and liberty. Economic sanctions are really a "feel good" approach to promoting human rights without any chance of being effective. Indeed, sanctions antagonize the governments of target countries and radicalize those in power.

In contrast to the "feel good" approach of sanctions, the logic of trade liberalization posits a close link between increasing economic freedom and securing human rights. Unlike sanctions, trade liberalization weakens the power of government and civilizes nations. The institutional infrastructure of a market system is supportive of personal freedom and good government. Free markets, based on private property and consent, encourage individual responsibility, self-esteem, social mobility, and tolerance—all of which are associated with human rights and democracy. . . .

ECONOMIC SANCTIONS WOULD NOT WORK

China's lack of respect for human rights, its use of political prisoners, and its failure to protect property rights (including those to intellectual property) stem primarily from the CCP's monopoly of power—a monopoly that rests on the idea that rights do not belong to the people but are privileges conferred by the state and can be taken away at any time. Yet, the fact that China is a bad government does not justify the use of sanctions to prevent legitimate trade. In the event that China uses slave or prison labor, or violates U.S. copyright laws, the U.S. would be justified in penalizing the rights' violators. . . . Before doing so, however, U.S. policymakers ought to consider the probability of success and consider alternative measures that may be more effective in the long run to change the nature of China's economic and political system.

In the case of China, economic sanctions have little chance of success. Although the United States accounts for more than 30 percent of China's export market, the threat of placing prohibitively high tariffs on a range of Chinese products is not politically feasible. American consumers would immediately see the higher prices and protest. Even if such a policy were politically feasible, it would be difficult to implement because China could transship products through Hong Kong or other countries, and U.S. customs officials would find it hard to identify the point of origin. Likewise, restricting American exports to China, which amounted to $11.7 billion in 1995, or curtailing the billions of dollars U.S. investors have poured into China would cause a political backlash from stakeholders and would be difficult to enforce.

But even if the U.S. government could block flows of goods and capital to China, there is no guarantee that other countries would not step in to fill the gap. Instead of buying from Boeing or looking to American investors, the Chinese would shift to Airbus Industrie and look to European and Asian trading partners for additional capital—and U.S. investors would try to reroute their funds into China rather than abandon their invested capital.

DEMOCRATIC DEVELOPMENT IN CHINA

Many are calling for the end of the extension of Most Favored Nation trading status and the imposition of tariffs on Chinese goods entering the United States. For the executive branch of the United States government, the primary formulator of our foreign policy, I believe this would be a mistake. As Americans we must never give up on the idealism of the Universal Declaration of Human Rights, but we must make sure that our long-term idealism is tempered by a short-term realism. It would be completely unrealistic to put all of our other foreign policy interests on hold in order to challenge the human rights record of a country from whom we need cooperation on such things as terrorism and nuclear proliferation, and which we also hope to influence in its movement toward a more democratic development.

David M. Abshire, *Vital Speeches of the Day*, September 15, 1997.

Finally, if America were to ban trade with China, China would retaliate. The ensuing trade war would harm both countries, as well as the Asian tigers, and do irreparable damage to the evolution of the market and civil society in China.

Monitoring the use of prison labor and tracing goods made by political prisoners in China would be difficult but not impossible. But even if the West were able to effectively monitor such activities, there is no guarantee that other countries would do the same. In fact, many countries have supported China against the United States when it comes to human rights. At the 52nd session of the U.N. Commission on Human Rights (April 1996), an attempt to pass a U.S. sponsored resolution critical of China's record on human rights—especially with regard to Tibet, the criminal justice system, and religious freedom—did not even get off the ground. China proposed a "no action" motion, meaning no discussion of the resolution and no vote on it. The motion passed by a vote of 27 to 20, with 6 countries (including Mexico, the Philippines, South Korea, and Russia—all major recipients of U.S. aid) abstaining. . . .

The foremost reason economic sanctions are unlikely to promote human rights in China is the resolve of the CCP. Hard-liners in the party will not tolerate any invasion of their stronghold of power, as the world witnessed in Tiananmen Square in 1989. They see sanctions as a capitalist tool designed to undermine China's rapid growth and weaken the CCP's hold on political power. Even if the sanctions disrupted economic life, they would have no lasting effect on China's political system—and may even serve to strengthen the ruling elite's resolve to promote communism at any cost. Closing China off from the outside world by means of sanctions would be more apt to play into the hands of the hard-liners than to overthrow them. . . .

The best strategy for the United States is to take steps to move China toward a market-liberal order. What China needs is a new system and a new way of thinking about human rights. Economic sanctions, as my colleague William Niskanen says, are rather like strategic bombing—they miss the main target but claim many innocent victims. Human rights will come to China only when property rights are treated as fundamental civil rights and when civil rights are protected by law. As Harry Wu, a former political prisoner in China, wrote in the *Washington Post* (26 May 1996), "Until private ownership is allowed on a wide scale, genuine liberalization—representative government, free markets and individual rights—will remain elusive" in China.

CREATING A MARKET-LIBERAL ORDER

To depoliticize economic life, China needs constitutional change and new thinking (xin si wei). Chinese scholar Jixuan Hu writes, "By setting up a minimum group of constraints and letting human creativity work freely, we can create a better society without having to design it in detail. That is not a new idea, it is the idea of law, the idea of a constitution."

As the world's leading constitutional democracy, the United States should spread its ethos of liberty by keeping its markets open and by extolling the principles that made it great. America should not play the dangerous game of pitting human rights activists against free traders. American prosperity and global prosperity are better served by open markets than by well-intended economic sanctions. History has shown that the best route to freedom and prosperity is market liberalism not market socialism. China should be admitted to the World Trade Organization as soon as possible and be given unconditional most-favored-nation trade status, which should be renamed "normal trade relations."

Governments everywhere need to get out of the business of trade and leave markets alone. Western democratic governments, in particular, need to practice the principles of freedom they preach and recognize that free trade is not a privilege but a right.

"I question the . . . observation in the United States that trade and a hybrid form of capitalism will lead to democracy in China."

FREE TRADE DOES NOT PROMOTE HUMAN RIGHTS IN CHINA

Harry Wu

Harry Wu, who spent nineteen years as a political prisoner in China's forced labor camps, was eventually deported and granted asylum in the United States. He is the author of *Laogai—The Chinese Gulag* and *Bitter Winds*, an autobiography. In the following viewpoint, Wu argues that free trade will not improve the state of human rights in China. He contends that since China's capital is controlled by its government and military, free trade with Western countries is more likely to increase the power of the Chinese state rather than foster civil and political rights for individuals. In Wu's opinion, the United States and other countries should develop a policy of restraint toward China, including the use of some trade restrictions and the condemnation of China's prison labor camps.

As you read, consider the following questions:

1. How does the Chinese government strengthen its appeal to the Chinese people, according to Wu?
2. In the author's opinion, what lesson did Chinese leaders learn from the massacre in Tiananmen Square?
3. Why is there a need for more international news broadcasts in China, in Wu's opinion?

Reprinted from Harry Wu, "The Need to Restrain China," *Journal of International Affairs*, vol. 49, no. 2 (Winter 1996), by permission of the *Journal of International Affairs* and the Trustees of Columbia University in the City of New York. Minor edits were made to accommodate length and format requirements.

Before the collapse of the Soviet Union, the American strategy was to use China as a wildcard in the Cold War, though the usefulness of playing Beijing off of Soviet interests is no more. Now there is a serious question whether the United States has any real policy toward China, other than supporting the interests of American business. U.S. objectives in China seem to be driven more by quarterly profit considerations, access to cheap labor and wishful thinking about the buying potential of over a billion Chinese. This is made all the more possible by Deng Xiaoping's policy of implementing so-called market reforms. [Deng Xiaoping was the paramount leader of China from 1978 until his death in February 1997.] Deng, recognizing the complete failure of communism to provide a better life for the average Chinese, frequently said he did not care if the cat was white or black, so long as it caught mice. America, along with the rest of the world, seems intent on providing the cheese.

AN ECONOMIC AND POLITICAL GIANT

American policy makers and analysts are constantly reminding everyone who will listen that China will soon have the largest economy in the world. What seems to be lacking in this discussion is anything about the implications of an economic giant also growing into a political and military mammoth. It seems silly to think that an economic giant will be a political and military midget. Every analyst who knows anything about China knows that communism as an ideology has been dead for some time. The Chinese people were the first to know this, but the Party leadership learned the truth some years ago. Deng, with his program of reforms, had this insight before anyone else in the party leadership.

But the Party remains in power and is intent upon maintaining power as it continues to transform itself into something new. There is only one choice open to the party leadership in this transformation. They must portray themselves as patriots and nationalists. Reaching back into history, they know they can appeal to the people by reminding them of how foreigners have exploited, insulted and abused China for centuries.

The ideological rhetoric which is produced by various government organs has been changing from communist to nationalist, both in tone and substance, for some time. There is no more talk about liberation or building the socialist paradise, but rather constant lectures about patriotic values and national self-respect. The cloak of nationalism now drapes every government power entity—the military, the police, judicial organs, even the *laogai* (labor camp) system. Schools have even shed talk of class struggle and socialist revolution.

Take my own experience as an example. Nearly forty years ago, I was condemned as an anti-communist, anti-popular, anti-socialist, bourgeois, counter-revolutionary rightist for criticizing the Soviet invasion of Hungary and the Party's treatment of ordinary citizens. Now I am simply branded a criminal who steals state secrets and passes them on to hostile foreign organizations. The criticism I have received recently from some Chinese around the world is further evidence of how the appeal to nationalism works. I am condemned for criticizing the motherland and being a tool of the foreigners. . . .

CHINA'S REPRESSIVE MACHINERY

The leaders of the Chinese Communist Party have started to walk down a road on which they can not turn back, though they are operating on a number of assumptions which may be valid for the foreseeable future. One assumption is that having suffered for so long, the people are more interested in their own economic development than in freedom and democracy. Another is that Party members want to remain in positions of power. A third is that the United States and other industrial countries are so concerned with their own economic well-being that they do not care about human rights, or freedom and democracy in China. They articulate this by saying that stability must be maintained in China at all costs. Therefore, the Party's assumption is that they can continue to repress all forms of dissent, and other countries will turn a blind eye. Another assumption critical to the outcome of the internal power struggle is the leadership's ability to modernize the People's Liberation Army and begin to project its force in Asia without significant resistance by the United States.

The issue of repression and human rights concerns me on a daily basis, of course, more than anything else. The Chinese government learned a very important lesson from the 1989 Tiananmen massacre. They learned that if they repress pro-democracy, religious and worker activists before they organize into larger groups and communicate with each other, the world will be silent about it, and it will not affect any nation's policy toward China. They also now understand a little better, after the Tiananmen demonstrations, the power of international television.

They also understand that it is child's play to circumvent any effort to deny them the means to modernize their repressive machinery. Again, my own experience is somewhat instructive.

As a result of foreign trade, even remote border outposts have sophisticated computers. Every one of the secret police agents guarding me had a Motorola cellular telephone. The People's Armed Police in Xinjiang had Cherokee-type jeeps. If anyone thinks that the Chinese police are ineffective let me tell you that they found nearly every taxi driver I used during my six-week trip in 1994.

Reprinted by permission of Joe Sharpnack.

They hate what the Laogai Research Foundation has done to reveal the ugly truth about the laogai—China's gulag—including further documentation of the use of executed prisoner's organs for transplants. They hate having to take the forced labor product trade underground. It has been made somewhat more difficult, though not impossible, to gather hard currency for this repressive machinery of the party. For putting them at this disadvantage, it really bothered them to let me go.

TRADE DOES NOT PROMOTE DEMOCRACY

So it should not be surprising that I question the underlying and often articulated observation in the United States that trade and a hybrid form of capitalism will lead to democracy in China. In my view, it is more likely to lead to the creation of a new form of a totalitarian, super-nationalistic military state. Even Fidel Castro has embraced the Chinese model in the hope that it will weaken American opposition to his regime.

The leaders of the Chinese Communist Party are certainly inventive in their effort to survive. Deng created what is most accurately called bureaucratic capitalism. It is a bastardized form of free market reforms designed to keep the reins of political and economic power in the hands of the current ruling elite. State-run companies are raising money in international capital markets, not truly private ones. The entrepreneurs are often party officials or their sons and daughters. Private property, the underpinning of capitalism, does not exist. Certainly property is being sold, but a close examination of who benefits reveals it is government and Party officials and state-controlled companies.

The many hundreds of Chinese companies in the West often appear to be private, but in reality are owned by the government. Spin-offs, break-ups and sales of state enterprises taking place in China today often end up in the hands of high-level officials, their relatives and others favored for one reason of power or another. If and when democracy comes to China, sorting out the real ownership will be a difficult but important task of the new government.

THE TRUTH ABOUT "PRIVATE BUSINESS"

Those in the West who are real capitalists are quick to embrace these changes as significant because they want to share in the process. They want to profit from the changes and could care less about the effect such reforms have on entrenching those currently in power. Like the British imperialists of old, they harbor great dreams of riches by selling products to China's huge populace.

U.S. businessmen and government officials, during most-favored-nation debates, used to extol the many "private" joint ventures being formed and were quick to say they could not be using forced labor because they knew who they were dealing with in these factories. Then some members of Congress proposed sanctions on Chinese military companies. All of a sudden both American officials and businessmen claimed they did not know the true ownership of the companies they were doing business with every day. This latter admission is far closer to the truth. In fact, with the exception of small business flourishing in China's cities, there is little real private business. The bulk of the country's capital remains in the hands of the party and government, including the military. Distinctions between and among these entities are more academic than real.

A POLICY OF RESTRAINT

So what are the United States' policy choices? Should America develop a policy of containment as some have argued, or should it simply follow an ad hoc policy of engagement as the Clinton administration believes? Or should the United States and other nations develop a policy of restraint towards China?

Containment in the old Cold War sense is unthinkable. The world of superpower politics is history. Engagement as practiced by the United States and the industrial countries seems little more than mercantilism at the moment.

Much of my thought is based on the historical belief that more or less democratic countries are not as likely as autocratic or totalitarian states to cause problems to their neighbors, and therefore to the rest of this small world. At the moment, our policy should be characterized by restraint and we should urge restraint upon the Chinese government. The United States and other countries can begin to develop a policy of restraint in the following ways:

1. Making clear to the Chinese Communist Party that its repression of dissidents will have real, not just rhetorical, costs. Some form of linkage to trade and economic assistance is appropriate, even if the issue of most-favored-nation trading status is dead. For instance, there is no defensible reason why the United States and Western democracies should permit companies owned and run by the People's Armed Police and the People's Liberation Army to operate in their countries. There is also no reason why China should be the largest customer of the World Bank, when needy and much more democratic developing countries are neglected.

2. Condemning the continued existence of the *laogai*, instead of continuing to make believe it is just a simple prison system. This can be done through international organizations as well as national legislatures and parliaments. Regarding the latter, enforceable anti-forced labor laws can be written which punish Chinese trading companies.

3. All Chinese acts which violate international norms such as the sale of missile and nuclear technology should be immediately sanctioned, not swept under the rug. A consistent response is necessary if the United States is going to have any credibility with the Chinese and end this danger to international peace.

4. The legitimate demands of the people of Taiwan, Tibet and Hong Kong to determine their own future should be respected and supported, and linked to other aspects of U.S. policy. In the case of Taiwan, the United States must make it very clear that the cost to the Chinese of the use of force will be extremely high.

5. Once and for all, the Chinese argument that human rights are not universal should be condemned in meaningful ways. The

trial and sentencing of Wei Jingsheng is a classic example of the Chinese leadership taking advantage of the mercantilist impulses of the United States and other nations in their current policy formulations. Sacrificing the courageous at the altar of profit has no place in U.S. policy.

6. Prohibitions on the sale of technology and equipment to China which can be used by the military and/or police apparatus should be continued and expanded.

7. Based upon the belief that real change will only be brought about by the Chinese themselves, international broadcasts into China should be expanded greatly. Honest and accurate information is something average Chinese citizens need in order to make decisions, and they are not getting it.

THE NEED TO RE-EXAMINE U.S. POLICY

Changes are taking place in China, but these changes are being forced from the top without any meaningful say by the people. These changes cannot be simply managed by former communist bureaucrats. If this continues there will be real instability in China, and U.S. interests will be damaged.

China can develop its own form of democratic institutions over time in a peaceful way, but not, in my view, by repressing the legitimate aspirations of its people. In a truly ironic sense, U.S. policy which is aimed at maintaining a stable China will result in a more unstable China. History is replete with examples of the United States trying to prop up dictators who have lost their legitimacy with their own people. Unless we re-examine our policies, I fear we are headed for disaster in our relationship with China.

PERIODICAL BIBLIOGRAPHY

The following articles have been selected to supplement the diverse views presented in this chapter. Addresses are provided for periodicals not indexed in the *Readers' Guide to Periodical Literature*, the *Alternative Press Index*, the *Social Sciences Index*, or the *Index to Legal Periodicals and Books*.

Nick Alexander	"Missing Pieces," *Z Magazine*, September 1997.
Ben Barber	"Feeding Refugees, or War? The Dilemma of Humanitarian Aid," *Foreign Affairs*, July/August 1997.
Skip Barry	"Taking Aim at Child Slavery," *Dollars & Sense*, July/August 1997.
George Black	"Lower the Decibel Level on Human Rights," *Los Angeles Times*, March 10, 1997. Available from Reprints, Times Mirror Square, Los Angeles, CA 90053.
Charles Fairchild	"How to Get Cheap Shoes in a Global Economy: The Sweatshops' Media Spin Doctors," *Against the Current*, July/August 1997.
Stephen Glass	"The Young and the Feckless," *New Republic*, September 8 and 15, 1997.
Bob Herbert	"A Good Start," *New York Times*, April 14, 1997.
Index on Censorship	"Communicating Human Rights," January/February 1996.
Robert Kagan	"China Deserves Sanctions," *Washington Post National Weekly Edition*, June 23, 1997. Available from Reprints, 1150 15th St. NW, Washington, DC 20071.
David Masci	"Assisting Refugees: Do Current Aid Policies Add to the Problems?" *Congressional Quarterly*, February 7, 1997. Available from 1414 22nd St. NW, Washington, DC 20037.
Robert A. Senser	"To End Sweatshops: Workers' Rights in a Global Economy," *Commonweal*, July 18, 1997.
Victoria L. Sharp and Douglas Shenson	"Humanitarianism Under the Gun," *JAMA*, July 9, 1997. Available from 515 N. State St., Chicago, IL 60610.

CHAPTER 4

HOW SHOULD THE WORLD RESPOND TO CRIMES AGAINST HUMANITY?

CHAPTER PREFACE

After World War II, the Geneva and Genocide conventions were drafted to establish international agreement on outlawing torture, genocide, and crimes against humanity. Many in the international community, however, have questioned the effectiveness of these conventions, particularly in light of the genocides that occurred in the former Yugoslavia and Rwanda in the early 1990s. Some contend that the UN-proposed International Criminal Court (ICC), which could be established as early as 1998, would better address the problem of crimes against humanity by providing a permanent world tribunal in which to prosecute suspected perpetrators of genocide and war crimes.

Supporters argue that a permanent world criminal court is needed because national court systems are too often unwilling to prosecute individuals for massive human rights violations. Furthermore, they contend, temporary international tribunals, such as the ones formed after the resolutions of conflicts in Bosnia and Rwanda, take too long to set up and are often hampered by legal inexperience and financial problems. Proponents assert that establishing a permanent world court would ensure high-quality trials, swifter justice, and stronger deterrence against genocide and human rights violations. According to George Washington University law professor Thomas Buergenthal, who testified in favor of a permanent ICC before a 1993 Senate Foreign Relations Committee, "the existence of an international court is no guarantee that crimes [against humanity] will never again be committed, but it is sure to prevent some of them, and that in itself would be progress."

Opponents claim, however, that a permanent court would not facilitate efforts to prosecute human rights violators. Former State Department adviser Edwin D. Williamson, for example, argues that a permanent court would do nothing to solve what he calls "the greatest problem"—getting the criminals in custody. Others maintain that a permanent ICC could thwart a nation's efforts to establish calm after a civil war. Some countries offer amnesties to warring groups after civil conflicts in an attempt to create national reconciliation, and such endeavors would be undermined by requiring war criminals to be tried in a permanent world court, critics contend.

The question of how to prevent genocide and crimes against humanity continues to foster controversy. The authors in the following chapter offer several opinions on this troubling subject.

"The International Criminal Court
will be good for America, and it will
be good for the world."

A PERMANENT INTERNATIONAL
CRIMINAL COURT SHOULD BE
CREATED

Jimmy Carter

A permanent world criminal court should be established to prosecute suspected perpetrators of genocide and crimes against humanity, argues Jimmy Carter in the following viewpoint. In his opinion, temporary tribunals, such as the ones created in response to war crimes committed in Rwanda and Bosnia, are hampered by financial difficulties and faulty investigative procedures. According to Carter, a permanent international court would help to ensure speedier, effective, and bias-free trials. Former U.S. president Jimmy Carter chairs the Atlanta-based Carter Center, which works to promote peace and human rights worldwide.

As you read, consider the following questions:

1. How has the Bosnia tribunal made its investigations more effective, according to Carter?
2. How could the international community improve the functioning of the Rwanda and Bosnia tribunals, in the author's opinion?
3. In Carter's opinion, what is wrong with the proposal to give the UN Security Council control over the procedures of a permanent international criminal court?

Reprinted from Jimmy Carter, "A World Criminal Court Is Urgently Needed," *Los Angeles Times*, December 10, 1996, by permission of the Los Angeles Times Syndicate; ©1996 Los Angeles Times.

Out of the horrors of World War II, world leaders collectively agreed that genocide and crimes against humanity represented a threat to international peace and security, above and beyond the populations directly affected. To avert future occurrences, mechanisms were devised, such as the Geneva and Genocide conventions, which place obligations on states engaged in warfare and the international community at large. Unfortunately, these have been inadequate in their ability to enforce state compliance. Genocide has been perpetrated twice within the last few years, in the former Yugoslavia and Rwanda.

ADDRESSING CRIMES AGAINST HUMANITY

Political efforts to address these crises failed for far too long. World leaders have been largely divided about what could have been done to prevent them, given the absence of enforceable protection procedures. One response to this concern has been the creation of special tribunals to prosecute the architects of genocidal policies and practices in the two countries.

Simultaneously, negotiations have been under way within the United Nations to create an International Criminal Court. This would be a permanent court for prosecuting suspected perpetrators of crimes against humanity when national courts are not able to do so, eliminating the need for special tribunals. In November 1996, these negotiations resulted in a landmark agreement to convene a diplomatic conference in 1998, during which a treaty establishing the court would be concluded.

These developments offer hope in the struggle to protect human rights, but will require greater care and attention in the coming years.

SPECIAL TRIBUNALS FACE PROBLEMS

Since the creation of the two special tribunals, they have been marred with difficulties that provide lessons for the permanent court. Early on, financial resources were scarce. While this lack seems to have been solved for the time being, other matters threaten the tribunals' effectiveness.

After initial missteps, the Bosnia Tribunal has gradually addressed many of these issues, including performing more effective investigations of crimes of sexual violence against women. This required proper definitions of crimes in international law, adequate specialized training and arrangements for collection of evidence and testimonies as well as witness protection.

However, more general problems, such as failure to arrest and extradite the vast majority of these indicted by the tribunal, could undermine its prospects for successful prosecutions.

The Rwanda Tribunal suffers from more acute problems, including shortages of qualified personnel, limited training, faulty methodology and weak investigative procedures. The matter of investigating crimes of sexual violence against women has not been handled well and needs dedicated resources and expertise. In addition to indictments having been slow in emerging, as of December 1996 only three of the 21 of those indicted are in the custody of the Tribunal.

THE BENEFITS OF AN INTERNATIONAL CRIMINAL COURT

By enforcing international law in a fair and consistent manner, the International Criminal Court (ICC) would serve to deter future war crimes and crimes against humanity, and therefore lessen the necessity for U.S. intervention in such cases as Bosnia and Somalia. These types of interventions can prove to be costly and often dangerous. When a conflict has happened, justice to victims, survivors, and their families promotes reconciliation, thus hastening peace and shortening the time needed for international intervention.

World Federalist Association ICC Project, September 1997.

The responsibility falls upon the international community to ensure the effective functioning of the tribunals by investing in them resources and political will that until now, have fallen short of what is needed. One place to start is for all nations to enact laws that enable them to extradite indicted war criminals to The Hague.

THE NEED FOR A PERMANENT COURT

The permanent court is needed so that any future cases can be brought forward quickly without waiting years for procedures and structures to be built, as has been the case with the special tribunals. Now that a date has been set for the court's establishment, the U.S. government should play a leadership role in ensuring that it will be constituted in a way that enables it to work independently from political pressures. We should reflect on our own experience which shows that a judicial process must not be vulnerable to politics or personal preferences. It must be guided by the law alone.

In that light, a U.S. proposal to grant the Security Council control over prosecutions in the court would undermine its very purpose. Such a move rightly would be seen by many nations as a means for serving only the interests of the permanent members of the Security Council rather than as an independent arbiter of justice.

The court will not be a panacea. As we have found in our own society, a criminal justice system does not ensure the absence of violence, but we would never consider eliminating it as a key ingredient in any strategy to protect civil rights and public safety in general.

The International Criminal Court will be good for America, and it will be good for the world. Meanwhile, all nations should consider it their duty to ensure that the existing tribunals overcome current difficulties and complete their work as expeditiously and effectively as possible.

"[The proposed Permanent
International Criminal Court] is
bold and noble in conception, but
promises wretched results."

A PERMANENT INTERNATIONAL CRIMINAL COURT WOULD BE COUNTERPRODUCTIVE

Bruce Fein

In the following viewpoint, Bruce Fein argues that creating a permanent international criminal court to address genocide and crimes against humanity would be counterproductive. According to Fein, international criminal courts have been ineffective, unsuccessful, and unfairly influenced by the politics of powerful nations. Furthermore, he argues, the threat of criminal prosecutions by a permanent world court could damage a nation's efforts to establish peace after a civil war. Fein is a lawyer and freelance writer specializing in legal issues.

As you read, consider the following questions:

1. In the author's opinion, in what way have the war crimes tribunals for the former Yugoslavia mocked justice?
2. According to Fein, what political bias was evident in the Nuremberg trials?
3. What kinds of violence might be considered morally justifiable, in Fein's opinion?

Reprinted from Bruce Fein, "Debasing the Law," *Washington Times*, December 24, 1996, by permission of the *Washington Times*.

A s H.L. Mencken reputedly quipped, there is a simple answer to every complex question, and it is wrong. And so it is with the simple-minded international initiative to enshrine a Permanent International Criminal Court (ICC) as an immaculate crusader for human rights. It is bold and noble in conception, but promises wretched results.

The heart-wrenching genocides in Bosnia and Rwanda occasioned ad hoc War Crimes Tribunals for the Former Yugoslavia and Rwanda under the aegis of the United Nations Security Council. Neither has proven inspiring. Only a handful of the 75 indictees in the case of the former Yugoslavia are in custody, and the chief culprits in genocide and war crimes, such as Bosnian Serbs Radovan Karadzac and Gen. Ratko Mladic, seem destined to defeat justice. A tiny number of their myrmidons may be punished, making a mockery of evenhanded justice. The Rwanda tribunal is an embarrassment to due process because of scarce and primitive legal talent and resources.

THE FAILURES OF INTERNATIONAL TRIBUNALS

The archvillains of the Bosnian atrocities are receiving kid-glove treatment by North Atlantic Treaty Organization (NATO) countries for reasons of state. It is thought that if a muscular approach were taken to apprehending politically powerful indictees, the Dayton peace accords would unravel, civil war would reignite, and Bosnia would be partitioned between Serbia and Croatia with a rump state left for Bosnian Muslims. That subordination of international law to Realpolitik fits the Post–World War II precedents set at Nuremberg and Tokyo like a glove, and is inevitable in any event.

At Nuremberg, the United States, Great Britain and France were anxious to avoid a confrontation with the Soviet Union. The Cold War was not yet a fixture of the international scene, the Yalta accords pledging democratic freedoms in Eastern and Central Europe had not yet been subverted, and substantial numbers of Allied prisoners of war (POWs) were under the control of the ruthless Josef Stalin and the Red Army. The Nuremberg prosecutors thus whitewashed indisputable Soviet war crimes indistinguishable from those charged against several Nazi defendants. The latter were accused and convicted of plotting and conducting aggressive warfare. That accusation perfectly describes Soviet attacks on Poland, the Baltic States, Finland and Romania after concluding the odious Ribbentrop-Molotov Pact. Even more outrageous, Nazis were indicted for allegedly perpetrating the Katyn Forest massacre of Polish officers, although

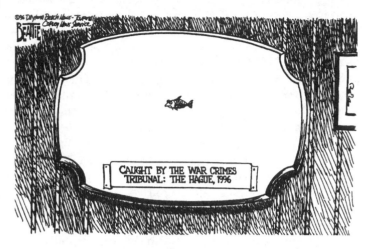

Bruce Beattie. Reprinted by permission of Copley News Service.

"Uncle Joe" had ordered the carnage to reduce Poland to postwar impotence.

At Tokyo, Emperor Hirohito escaped indictment for such war crimes as the Pearl Harbor aggression, the Rape of Nanking, and the Bataan Death March because the Japanese deity featured prominently in Gen. Douglas MacArthur's occupation and reconciliation plans.

MIGHT MAKES RIGHT

To believe that Permanent ICC would purge the prosecution and trial of war crimes of the glaring injustices of Realpolitik is to believe in fantasyland. It is contemplated that its jurisdiction would reach at least genocide, significant war crimes, and crimes against humanity whether or not an international conflict was implicated. These legal concepts, however, invite Machiavellian manipulation in a world where "might makes right" is the norm, not the exception. Some Bosnian Serbs have been indicted by the ad hoc Yugoslav tribunal for indiscriminate shelling of civilians during the siege of Sarajevo. Comparable civilian casualties have been registered in Chechnya, Kashmir and East Timor at the hands of Russian, Indian and Indonesian forces, respectively. Would you bet a ruble or rupee on ultimate war crimes accountability of any of the three nations by a Permanent ICC? Would it call Communist China to account for attempting the complete eradication of Tibetan culture and customs?

Pol Pot commits genocide in Cambodia, his chief lieutenant Ieng Sary receives a royal pardon, and the international community yawns.

THE THREAT TO NATIONAL NEGOTIATIONS

Realpolitik will also infect determinations of whether otherwise indictable offenses are non-culpable because morally justified. History is instructive. French Revolutionaries attempted genocide against the nobility during the Terror to avenge centuries of brutal oppression. John Brown attempted a slave insurrection and the killings of white slaveowners and their families to rid the United States of an unspeakable scourge. Members of the African National Congress terrorized white civilians in South Africa to end apartheid. Whether such violence was criminal or heroic will be hotly contested for the ages, and judgments will bristle with political, racial and cultural biases. Would Tibetans be guilty of genocide if they indiscriminately slaughtered Han Chinese in their territory?

In some cases, a Permanent ICC might menace the termination of bloody civil wars. Governments and rebel groups frequently agree to end hostilities conditional on mutual amnesties for "political" offenses that might be indictable by the ICC. Guatemala is a recent example, and similar amnesties have been negotiated in South Africa, Chile, Argentina and El Salvador. These types of arrangements in furtherance of peace and national reconciliation would be problematic if a war crimes prosecution before the ICC hung like a Sword of Damocles over the warring parties.

The rule of law is weakened, not strengthened, when employed as an instrument of Realpolitik. That breeds cynicism, resentment and worse. It is preferable to confine the law to areas where evenhanded application of transcendent principles of justice has at least a fighting chance. Many ugly injustices will escape with only moral censure, but at least they will be denied any claim of legal indifference, exoneration or blessing.

"We cannot assume that only sick people or even socially marginal or alienated people will do evil."

INVESTIGATING HUMAN CRUELTY MAY PREVENT FUTURE ATROCITIES

Fred E. Katz

To help prevent future genocides and crimes against humanity, the human capacity for cruelty must be seriously investigated, argues Fred E. Katz in the following viewpoint. He contends that scientific study may lead to important insights about why normal and healthy human beings occasionally commit horrendous deeds. A fuller understanding of the interplay of social psychology and morality may enable humanity to better control its propensity to commit inhumane acts, Katz concludes. Katz, author of *Ordinary People and Extraordinary Evil: A Report on the Beguilings of Evil*, has taught sociology at the University of Missouri, Johns Hopkins University, the University of Toronto, and Tel Aviv University.

As you read, consider the following questions:

1. What is an incremental process, according to Katz?
2. In what way did the German doctor Eduard Wirths participate in genocide, according to the author?
3. What are mutant moral communities, in Katz's opinion?

Reprinted from Fred E. Katz, "We Need Not Remain So Impotent," *Peace Review*, June 1996, by permission of Carfax Publishing Ltd., Oxfordshire.

When we hear of large-scale social horrors, new and old—some as serious as genocide—we are continually surprised. Yet being shocked is not good enough. And remembering is not good enough either. Let's face it, we do not have the tools to make sense of these horrors, or to understand them, let alone to end them. Intellectually, we are terribly impotent.

Our impotence comes from more than knowing that the horrors are really horrible. It results also from our scientific shortcomings: our inability thus far to devise a viable psychology that addresses such events. We suffer from a terrible failure of imagination. But this need not be the case.

We must develop a social psychology of human moral existence. To understand horrendous human behavior, we need not search for monsters or demons or even sickness and aberrations from normal human activity. Instead, the clues are waiting to be discovered in the common makeup of ordinary human beings.

We still have few insights into horrifying events such as genocide, mass murder, and organized mass torture. We have considerable information about such horrors: so much so that we often protect ourselves by becoming numb and unresponsive.

HUMANITY'S SCIENTIFIC SHORTCOMINGS

Rather than poor information, our shortsightedness stems instead from our scientific shortcomings—the innovative research by distinguished investigators such as Theodore Adorno, Stanley Milgram, Bruno Bettelheim, Robert Lifton and Ervin Staub, notwithstanding. Our impotence exists not only because, in some circumstances, we humans seem to be all too ready to commit horrors against our fellow-human beings. It also results from large gaps in our scientific work.

We have made progress. In recent years we have learned, thanks to the historian Christopher Browning, that when horrendous evil occurs we must consider the contribution made by "Ordinary Men." We cannot assume that only sick people or even socially marginal or alienated people will do evil. Well-adjusted, and apparently healthy and decent human beings can also participate in evil. Sometimes they participate most diligently and energetically.

ORDINARY PEOPLE AND EVIL DEEDS

Ordinary people's participation in horrors poses a distinctive challenge for us. It would be much easier if we were dealing only with "sick" or "disorderly" people. Then we'd merely need to discover the nature of their sickness or disorder. But when horrible deeds occur at the hands of people who are not identifiably sick, it obliges us to reexamine what we mean by human ordinariness.

People's ordinary, humdrum daily behavior can be harnessed for doing extraordinarily evil deeds—just as readily as it can be harnessed for doing extraordinarily good deeds. Scholars and scientists must discover how this actually works. We need an approach that does more than simply assume that pathological actions must be based on pathological causes; that only distinctive flaws in one's makeup (or in a society's makeup) can produce morally flawed actions. We must go beyond, for example, Theodore Adorno's quest for distinctive attributes, such as an authoritarian personality, as a way of explaining what predisposes people to do horrible deeds when an authority figure demands them.

In more contemporary thinking, we often try to explain horrendous behavior by looking for distinctive cultural markers—such as the denigration of particular ethnic groups—that seem to lead members of one ethnic group onto a path of horror against the members of another. Historical circumstances such as ethnic denigrations have doubtlessly played a part. Recently, in Bosnia and in Rwanda, ethnic stereotypes and long-standing ethnic animosities were surely among the ingredients—perhaps even the catalysts or rationalizations—for terror campaigns against innocent members of certain ethnic groups. Besides Bosnia and Rwanda, they may well exist elsewhere as well.

BENIGN BEHAVIOR CAN LEAD TO BRUTALITY

Yet we must concentrate on ordinariness—even the ordinariness of recognizing that an ethnic denigration may not have begun in outright hatred of one ethnic group toward another one. Instead, it may have begun as individuals matter-of-factly and without malice identify small ways that one's own ethnic group differs from other ethnic groups. Such benign beginnings can culminate in massively brutal actions. This can take place through a sequence of small, localized acts—each one addressing an immediate problem—that become cumulatively ever-more extreme in their hostility toward other groups, even when they did not begin with any deliberate decision to do violence against the other.

These "incremental processes" can be seen when we examine phenomenon as different as the Nazi movement and the personal careers of American professionals. For the former, the genocidal "Final Solution" was not spelled out at the beginning. It emerged through an incremental process of ever-more severe restrictions, and ever-greater persecutions, directed against the victims. Having established its direction, however, an incremental process can gain momentum toward ever-greater inhumane activity. It may gain an internal momentum, where little or no outside prodding is needed to escalate into murderous behavior against groups designated as "enemies."

ORDINARY GERMANS AND THE HOLOCAUST

Contrary to what is commonly believed, the Germans who executed Jews were not exclusively a select group of Nazi fanatics, not only members of the SS but also tens of thousands of ordinary Germans from all walks of life. . . .

The number of Germans working in concentration camps, ghettos, police battalions and other institutions involved in the genocide was far greater than people realize. Although a definitive estimate is difficult to make, it is clear that in excess of 100,000 Germans, and probably far more, helped exterminate European Jews.

Daniel Jonah Goldhagen, New York Times, March 17, 1996.

This process may have an inner consistency and, in the eyes of the participants, an inner moral consistency, so that people who commit horrors against members of other ethnic groups do so believing they're doing the right and noble and good thing. Ethnic markers—be they malignant or benign—can be woven from the cloth of the ordinariness of everyday living. We can understand more about how this cloth is being woven.

THE SIGNIFICANCE OF "FOLLOWERS"

Ervin Staub tells us that not only leaders but also "followers" must be seen as active contributors to massive evil. In addition, we must concentrate on how followers not only "follow" leaders, but on how they often make major contributions of their own to social horrors, sometimes going well beyond the demands and specifications set forth by the leaders. We must look at how these followers may transform genocidal fantasies by leaders into actual programs of action. In this process, entirely decent, humane and courageous people can become ardent participants in evil, even in genocide.

The Nazi Doctors, Robert Jay Lifton's case study of the German Dr Eduard Wirths, demonstrated this most starkly. One of the first things the Nazis did when they came to power in Germany in 1933 was to restrict how Jewish physicians could practice medicine. These restrictions became increasingly extreme until, in 1938, Jewish physicians lost their medical accreditation altogether. German Christian physicians became more and more reluctant to treat Jews, thus increasingly depriving them of medical care.

Dr Eduard Wirths was a Christian physician. He practiced medicine in a small community. He was known as a very competent, decent, humane and caring human being. He had Jews come to him in secret, at night, to receive medical treatment. Sometimes he treated them for injuries they suffered from being beaten by Nazi ruffians. By treating Jews, Dr Wirths was placing himself and his family at risk, but he accepted the consequences.

A few years later, in 1942 and 1943, the extermination of Jews in places like the Auschwitz concentration camp was in full swing. The "selections" of who would die right away and who would live a bit longer were carried out by physicians. Most of us have heard enough to envisage Dr Josef Mengele, standing on the ramp, coldly and flamboyantly making life and death decisions.

But which physician supervised Mengele? Who was in charge of the selection process? Who was the chief physician at Auschwitz? It was Dr Wirths. A decent, humane individual could participate in genocide; and participate not merely as a little underling who obeys orders. Such a person could, and did, become a major contributor to genocide.

The Practice of Evil

My 1993 book *Ordinary People and Extraordinary Evil* does not examine Wirths. But it does show how ordinary human ways can be harnessed for doing evil—how the doers of the most colossal evil (such as Rudolf Hoess, the chief of Auschwitz) can do so by harnessing the human ordinariness of their own makeup. We can understand evil-doing through "situational" psychology, which focuses on how people adapt to the evil situations in which they find themselves. The adaptations resemble those used in everyday life. They are not peculiar to evil-doing. But they can be used for evil-doing.

The practice of evil can be very beguiling because it will likely be nurtured within the confines of a distinctive habitat: within a local moral universe. The sociologist Emile Durkheim long ago taught us that societies are primarily moral communities. We humans obtain our fundamental sense of self—who we are, what we are—from our membership in moral communities. Within large societies there are many sub-societies—intimate groups, families, formal and informal associations. These are also moral communities, from which we obtain our sense of ourselves as human beings, what we are here for, the purpose and meaning of our life.

But we're not lumps of inert moral protoplasm, who merely receive moral instructions from our moral community. To the contrary, we are continually interpreting, refining and adapting the moral instructions we receive. In these ways, we tend to be active members of our moral community at the same time as we, ongoingly, create our personal moral life. Yet we do so in our community's shadow.

DEPARTURES FROM EXISTING MORAL SYSTEMS

Ours is a world where there sometimes also emerge mutant moral communities. They are mutants from existing moral systems. They arise from an existing moral community and share some of its component parts. For example, the mutant Nazi German system shared a good deal with pre-Nazi German culture. But mutations can also drastically depart from the existing moral heritage.

For example, the Nazis obtained the loyalty and cooperation of many German physicians in committing eugenic murders of people with mental impairments and genocidal actions against Jews and others viewed as threats to the Nazi credo. The Nazis did not ask physicians to renounce their fundamental medical commitment to being healers. Instead, they persuaded these physicians that, by joining the Nazi cause, they would become healers on a far deeper, more fundamental level. By contributing their medical skills to the Nazi cause they would become healers of the German nation, the German *Volk*, and the Nordic race. This proved very persuasive. Many physicians, including Wirths, accepted this reinterpretation of their commitment, seeing it as a glorious change, a revitalization of their profession. By accepting the Nazi message they would become even better physicians.

The Nazi mutation was so beguiling to physicians because it did not ask them to substitute a new commitment for their old one. Instead, it coopted an already strongly held commitment into a new shape that was integrated into the larger Nazi system of beliefs and objectives. This created a distinctive new arrangement of the German moral system where new priorities prevailed. Here, a physician's participation in mass killings seemed justified.

Tip O'Neill, the former Massachusetts Congressman, used to say that all politics is local. Morality seems to be local, too. Those who have committed genocidal actions in the Nazi era and in other eras (such as the recent ethnic cleansings in Bosnia) share a common trait beyond their horrifying acts: they are members of mutant moral communities yet their actions seem to be entirely justified (at least to them) in their own, local world.

MUTANT MORAL COMMUNITIES

The real world contains many communities that embody moral mutations, which sometimes depart drastically from the fundamental values most agree that all humans ought to share. Such mutations can be incorporated into a communal life that its members regard as most compelling.

The mutations can be woven into the fabric of distinct communities, with their own systems of rewards and constraints; their own formulas for achieving a worthy and noble life; their own visions of human destiny and human callings. The individual members of such mutant moral communities believe they're operating within a distinctive moral order, one that deserves their total allegiance and loyalty.

The size and shape of such a community varies. It may consist of an entire country, as in Germany during the Nazi era. Or it may transcend national boundaries. More usually, it consists of a sub-group within a country, such as a cult-like fringe group, or a city gang.

It's exasperating to find that mutant communities often seem to be impervious to the larger shared moral community. "Mutant" members no longer seem to understand the language or the messages of the broader human community. The appeals, the pleadings and warnings of the larger community are not only dismissed: They are so thoroughly reinterpreted—within the mutant community's warped perspective—that for all practical purposes, they are no longer heard.

Each mutant community comprises an entire universe—a world—within which the members see themselves living a full and significant life. They shun the outside world's offerings—its advice, suggestions, demands, and even its rewards. When they receive outside messages, these appeals are viewed as seductions, as hostile efforts to convert members to an alien outside world. The participating members of this local moral universe cannot understand why the outside world views their actions— such as the killing of Jews in Auschwitz or the killing of Muslims in the former Yugoslavia—as criminal behavior. Their own moral universe, in contrast, views these killings as noble, necessary, and as part of a sacred crusade to produce a better world.

When mutant moral communities arise, they powerfully affect human behavior precisely because they lay a moral claim upon their members. Moral communities can mold their members into "true believers" by serving as social support systems. They make the community's members deaf and blind to alternative perspectives. Members earnestly believe they are on the side of morality. They are defending a way of life. They're in the grasp of a destiny that cries out for implementation—where one's own actions are measured by a unique yardstick, one that assesses progress toward that destiny by criteria most of us find revolting. But to the members, these criteria are valid and totally compelling. They are so compelling that individual members are often willing to sacrifice their own lives, their children's lives, and the lives of the rest of us.

No Need for Despair

Despite this grim news, we can nevertheless take heart knowing that members of mutant communities are not people from Mars. Many of us, occasionally, live in a local moral universe. Many of us, occasionally, make our peace with mutant rearrangements of our moral commitments. From this we should derive hope not despair. Most likely people's attraction to morally compelling rearrangements occurs through ordinary human beings doing ordinary things. As suggested, it may happen through small incremental decisions, or through the beguilings of evil when it's offered to us as a revitalization of our existing commitments. By emphasizing the ordinary, future investigations can help us understand even better how moral rearrangements are produced. We may even learn to monitor and control them. We need to develop a social-psychology of human moral existence from which we may learn to become less impotent against the evil we humans so often inflict on one another.

| *"As the African proverb reminds us, 'truth is not always good to say.'"*

ATTEMPTS TO AMEND HUMAN RIGHTS VIOLATIONS WILL NOT ALLEVIATE SUFFERING

Michael Ignatieff

At the resolutions of wars and other conflicts involving crimes against humanity, societies often attempt to create justice and national atonement through trials, tribunals, and truth commissions. In the following viewpoint, Michael Ignatieff argues that there is no guarantee that tribunals will lead to national healing and reconciliation. On occasion such measures are effective, he points out. However, Ignatieff maintains, a nation's attempts to come to terms with its past by arriving at a commonly shared truth can fail because different groups' versions of the truth vary. Ignatieff is a freelance writer and journalist.

As you read, consider the following questions:

1. In what ways were the truth commissions in South America during the 1960s and 1970s effective, according to Ignatieff?
2. How are atrocity myths related to identity, in the author's opinion?
3. According to Ignatieff, what did the 1946 Nuremberg war-crimes trials fail to do?

Reprinted from Michael Ignatieff, "How Can Past Sins Be Absolved?" *World Press Review*, February 1997 (adapted from Michael Ignatieff, "Articles of Faith," *Index on Censorship*, September/October 1996), by permission of the author and the Index on Censorship.

W hat does it mean for a nation to come to terms with its past? Do nations, like individuals, have psyches? Can a nation's past make a people ill, as we know repressed memories sometimes make individuals ill? Conversely, can a nation or parts of it be reconciled to the past, as an individual can, by replacing myth with facts and lies with truth? Can we speak of nations "working through" a civil war or an atrocity as we speak of individuals working through a traumatic memory or event?

The International War Crimes Tribunal in The Hague is collecting evidence about atrocities in the former Yugoslavia. It is doing so not simply because such crimes against humanity must be punished—otherwise, international law means nothing—but also because establishing the truth about such crimes through the judicial process is held to be crucial to the eventual reconciliation of the people of the Balkans. In the African city of Arusha, a similar tribunal is collecting evidence about the genocide in Rwanda, believing likewise that truth, justice, and reconciliation are indissolubly linked in the rebuilding of shattered societies.

In both these instances, the rhetoric is noble but the rationale unclear. Justice in itself is not a problematic objective, but whether the attainment of justice always contributes to reconciliation is anything but evident. Truth, too, is a good thing, but as the African proverb reminds us, "truth is not always good to say."

TRUTH COMMISSIONS

In South Africa, Archbishop Desmond Tutu's Truth and Reconciliation Commission is collecting testimony from the victims and perpetrators of apartheid. In Tutu's own words, the aim is "the promotion of national unity and reconciliation . . . the healing of a traumatized, divided, wounded, polarized people." Laudable aims, but are they coherent? Look at the assumptions he makes: that a nation has one psyche, not many; that the truth is certain, not contestable; and that when it is known by all, it has the capacity to heal and reconcile. These are articles of faith about human nature: The truth is one, and if we know it, it will make us free.

Such articles of faith inspired the truth commissions in Chile, Argentina, and Brazil that sought to find out what had happened to the thousands of innocent people killed or tortured by the military juntas during the 1960s and 1970s. In all cases, the results were ambiguous. The truth commissions did succeed in establishing the facts about the disappearance, torture, and death of thousands of persons, and this allowed relatives and friends the consolation of knowing. At this individual level, the commissions did a power of good. But they were also told to generate a moral narrative—explaining the genesis of evil regimes and apportioning moral responsibility for their deeds.

The military, security, and police establishments were prepared to let the truth come out about individual cases of disappearance. But they fought tenaciously against prosecutions of their own people and against shouldering responsibility for their crimes. The military and police survived the inquisition with their legitimacy undermined but their power intact. The societies in question used the truth commissions to indulge in the illusion that they had put the past behind them. The truth commissions allowed exactly the false reconciliation with the past that they had been created to forestall.

TRUTH IS NOT SOCIAL REFORM

The dangers of this false reconciliation are real enough, but it is possible that disillusion with the truth commissions of Latin America goes too far. It was never in their mandate to transform the military and security apparatus, any more than it is in Archbishop Tutu's power to do the same. Truth is truth; it is not social or institutional reform.

Nor is it realistic to expect that when truth is proclaimed by an official commission it is likely to be accepted by the perpetrators. People, especially people in uniform, do not easily or readily surrender the premises upon which their lives are based. All that a truth commission can achieve is to reduce the number of lies that can be circulated unchallenged in public discourse. In Argentina, for example, it is now impossible to claim that the military did not throw half-dead victims into the sea from helicopters. Truth commissions can and do change public discourse and memory. They cannot be judged a failure because they fail to change behavior and institutions. That is not their function.

Truth commissions have the greatest chance of success in societies that have already created a powerful political consensus behind reconciliation, such as South Africa. In places like Yugoslavia, where the parties have murdered and tortured each other for years, the prospects for truth, reconciliation, and justice are much bleaker.

The idea that reconciliation depends on shared truth presumes that shared truth about the past is possible. But truth is related to identity. What you believe to be true depends, in some measure, on who you believe yourself to be. And that is mostly defined in terms of who you are not. To be a Serb is first and foremost not to be a Croat or a Muslim. If a Serb is someone who believes Croats have a historical tendency toward fascism, and a Croat is someone who believes Serbs have a penchant for genocide, then to discard these myths is to give up a defining element of their own identities. It is impossible to imagine the three sides ever agreeing on how to apportion responsibility and moral blame. The truth that matters to people is not factual or narrative truth, but moral or interpretive truth. And this will always be an object of dispute in the Balkans.

SOUTH AFRICA'S TRUTH COMMISSION

A moral order is too large and impalpable an aim to be achieved by any commission. Perhaps, at the beginning, the men and women of the South African Truth Commission thought they could draw a line under the past and turn to a clean page. But veterans of the process are now coming to terms with the fact that their work will never be over. Violence insinuated itself into the heart of the country's institutions, into each race's loyalty to its own. It will take generations to eliminate that violence, but at least now there is some measure of shared truth about it. It is just as well, perhaps, that South Africans have learned enough truth from the commission to never entirely trust their policemen—and each other—again.

Michael Ignatieff, *New Yorker*, November 10, 1997.

It is also an illusion to suppose that "impartial" or "objective" outsiders would ever succeed in getting their account of the catastrophe accepted by the parties to the conflict. The very fact of being an outsider discredits rather than reinforces legitimacy. The truth, if it is to be believed, must be proclaimed by those who have suffered its consequences.

Atrocity myths about the other side are an important part of the identities in question. Hill-country Serbs in the Foca region of Bosnia told British journalists in the summer of 1992 that their ethnic militias were obliged to cleanse the area of Muslims because it was a well-known fact that Muslims crucified Serbian children and floated their bodies down the river past Serbian settlements. This myth used to be spread about the Jews in medieval times. The myth was not true about the Jews and it is not true about Muslims, but that is not the point. The point is that myth is strangely impervious to facts. What is mythic is that atrocities are held to reveal the essential identity of the peoples in whose name they were committed. All the members of the group are held to have a genocidal propensity, even though atrocity can only be committed by individuals. The fiction at work here is akin to the nationalist delusion that the identities of individuals should be subsumed into their national identities. But nations are not like individuals: They do not have a single identity, conscience, or responsibility.

IS JUSTICE ARBITRARY?

The most important function of war-crimes trials is to "individualize" guilt, to relocate it from the collectivity to the individuals responsible. Yet trials inevitably fail to apportion all the guilt to all those responsible. Small fry pay the price for the crimes of the big fish, and this reinforces the sense that justice is arbitrary. Nor do such trials break the link between individual and nation. The 1946 war-crimes trials in Nuremberg failed to do this; the rest of the world still holds the Germans responsible collectively, and the Germans themselves still accept this responsibility. The most that can be said is that war-crimes trials do something to unburden a people of the fiction of collective guilt by helping them to transform guilt into shame. This appears to have happened in Germany, but it is not clear that Nuremberg itself accomplished this transformation of attitudes. As Ian Buruma has pointed out in The Wages of Guilt, many Germans dismissed the Nuremberg trials as nothing more than "victor's justice." It was not Nuremberg but the strictly German war-crimes trials of the 1960s that forced Germans to confront their part in the Holocaust. Verdicts reached in a German courtroom benefited from a legitimacy that the Nuremberg process never enjoyed.

It is open to question whether justice or truth actually heals. All societies, including our own, manage to function with only the most precarious purchase on the truth of their own past. Individuals may be made ill by repression of their own past, but it is less clear that what holds true for individuals must also hold true for societies. A society like Serbia, which allows well-established war criminals to hold public office and prevents them from being extradited to face international tribunals, may be a distasteful place to visit, but it is not necessarily a sick society. For such societies will not see themselves as sick but as healthy, refusing the outside world's iniquitous attempt to turn their heroes into criminals. War crimes challenge collective moral identities, and when these identities are threatened, denial is actually a defense of everything one holds dear.

There are many forms of denial, ranging from outright refusal to accept facts to complex strategies of relativization. Here one accepts the facts but argues that the enemy was equally culpable, or that the accusing party is also to blame, or that such "excesses" are regrettable necessities in war.

THE PAST IS LOCKED IN THE PRESENT

What seems apparent in the former Yugoslavia, in Rwanda, and in South Africa is that the past continues to torment because it is not really past. Reporters in the Balkan wars often reported that when they were told atrocity stories, they were occasionally uncertain whether these stories had occurred yesterday or in 1941 or 1841 or 1441. For the tellers of the tale, yesterday and today were the same. Crimes can never be safely fixed in the historical past; they remain locked in the present, crying out for vengeance.

This makes the process of coming to terms with the past, and of being reconciled to its painfulness, much more complicated than simply sifting fact from fiction, lies from truth. We know from victims of trauma that the mysterious inner work of the psyche is arduous. At first, the memory of trauma—a car crash, the death of a child or a parent—returns so frequently that it literally drives the present out. The victim lives in the past and suffers its pain over and over again. With time and reflection and talk, trauma takes its place in the past, and the pain becomes only a memory.

It is perilous to extrapolate from traumatized individuals to whole societies. It is simply an extravagant metaphor to think of societies coming awake from nightmare. The only coming awake that makes sense is one by one, individual by individual, in the recesses of their own identities. Nonetheless, individuals can be helped to heal and to reconcile by public rituals of atonement. When Chilean President Patricio Aylwin appeared on television to apologize to the victims of Augusto Pinochet's repression, he created the public climate in which a thousand acts of private repentance and apology became possible. He also symbolically cleansed the Chilean state of its association with these crimes.

THE FUTILITY OF VENGEANCE

The experience of the war in Yugoslavia makes it difficult to conceive of reconciliation in terms of "forgiving and forgetting," "turning the page," "putting the past behind us," and so on. The ferocity and scale of the war show up the hollowness of these clichés for what they are. But reconciliation might eventually be founded on something starker: the democracy of the dead, the equality of all victims, the drastic nullity of all struggles that end in killing, and the demonstrable futility of avenging the past in the present.

"The very survival of the Tibetans as a distinct people is under constant threat."

THE INTERNATIONAL COMMUNITY SHOULD INTERVENE ON BEHALF OF TIBET

Tenzin Gyatso

Various human rights organizations report that the people of Tibet face increasing religious repression and political persecution under Chinese colonial rule. In the following viewpoint, Tenzin Gyatso argues that such persecution amounts to an attempted cultural genocide of the Tibetan people. He contends that democratic countries must prompt Chinese leaders to commence honest negotiations with Tibetan authorities to achieve a peaceful resolution of the Tibetan-Chinese conflict. Gyatso is the fourteenth Dalai Lama—the spiritual leader of the Tibetan Buddhists. This viewpoint is excerpted from a speech he delivered before the British Parliament on July 16, 1996.

As you read, consider the following questions:

1. In what ways have the Chinese authorities persecuted the Tibetan people, according to Gyatso?
2. Why has the Dalai Lama adopted a "middle-way" approach to negotiations with China?
3. What four suggestions does Gyatso offer on Tibet's behalf to the world's democratic governments?

Reprinted from Tenzin Gyatso's speech, "Violations of Human Rights," London, July 16, 1996.

Today, the freedom struggle of the Tibetan people is at a crucial stage. In recent times the Chinese government has hardened its policies, increased repression in Tibet and resorted to bullying tactics in addressing the problems of Tibet. Observance of human rights in Tibet has, sadly, not improved. On the contrary, repression and political persecution have lately reached a new peak in Tibet. This has been documented in reports by various international human rights organisations.

CULTURAL GENOCIDE

Violations of human rights in Tibet have a distinct character. Such abuses are aimed at Tibetans as a people from asserting their own identity and their wish to preserve it. Thus, human rights violations in Tibet are often the result of institutionalised racial and cultural discrimination. If the human rights situation in Tibet is to be improved, the issue of Tibet should be addressed on its own merits. It should be seen as distinct from the overall situation in China. Undoubtedly, the Chinese in China suffer from human rights abuses, but these abuses are of an entirely different nature.

In Tibet our people are being marginalised and discriminated against in the face of creeping Sinocization. The destruction of cultural artefacts and traditions coupled with the mass influx of Chinese into Tibet amounts to cultural genocide. The very survival of the Tibetans as a distinct people is under constant threat. Similarly, the issues of environmental destruction and contamination, which have serious ramifications beyond the Tibetan plateau, and economic development must be addressed specifically with regard to Tibet. These problems are also different from those faced in China.

It is encouraging to note the growing concern being shown for the human rights situation in Tibet by many governments and non-governmental organizations (NGOs) around the world. A recent example of the growing international support for Tibet is the firm and principled stand taken by the Friedrich Naumann Foundation of Germany in the face of great pressure in co-sponsoring an international conference on Tibet in Germany in June 1996 and the adoption of a number of comprehensive and strongly worded resolutions by various parliaments around the world. But human rights' violations, environmental degradation and social unrest in Tibet are only the symptoms and consequences of a deeper problem. Fundamentally, the issue of Tibet is political. It is an issue of colonial rule: the oppression of Tibet by the People's Republic of China and resistance to that rule by the people of Tibet. This issue can be resolved only through negotiations and not, as China would have it, through force, intimidation, and population transfer.

A HISTORIC OPPORTUNITY

I am convinced that the next few years will be crucial in bringing about honest negotiations between us and the Chinese government. Such negotiations are the only way to promote a peaceful and comprehensive resolution of the Tibetan question. Moreover, the present situation offers a historic opportunity for the members of the international community to reassess their policy towards China, in order both to influence and to respond to the changes that are taking place in that country.

It is undoubtedly in the interest of the Chinese people that the present totalitarian one-party state gives way to a democratic system in which fundamental human rights and freedoms are protected and promoted. The people of China have clearly manifested their desire for human rights, democracy and the rule of law in successive movements starting in 1979 with the 'Democracy Wall' and culminating in the great popular movement of the spring of 1989.

China needs human rights, democracy and the rule of law. These values are the foundation of a free and dynamic society. They are also the source of true peace and stability. A society upholding such values will offer far greater potential and security for trade and investment. A democratic China is thus also in the interest of the international community in general and of Asia in particular. Therefore, every effort should be made not only to integrate China into the world economy, but also to encourage her to enter the mainstream of global democracy. Nevertheless, freedom and democracy in China can be brought about only by the Chinese themselves and not by anyone else. This is why the brave and dedicated members of the Chinese democracy movement deserve our encouragement and support.

SEEKING A PEACEFUL RESOLUTION

Democracy in China will have important consequences for Tibet. Many of the leaders of the Chinese democracy movement recognise that Tibetans have been ill-treated by Beijing and believe that such injustice should be redressed. Many of them openly state that Tibetans should be granted the opportunity to express and implement their right to self-determination. Even under the present one-party rule, China has undergone dramatic changes in the last 15, 16 years. These changes will continue. I remain optimistic that this transformation will make it possible for the Chinese leaders and encourage them to resolve the problem of Tibet peacefully through dialogue.

In the final analysis it is for the Tibetan and the Chinese peoples themselves to find a just and peaceful resolution to the Tibetan problem. Therefore, in our struggle for freedom and justice I have always tried to pursue a path of non-violence in order to ensure that a relationship based on mutual respect, friendship and genuine good neighbourliness can be sustained between our two peoples in the future. For centuries the Tibetan and the Chinese peoples have lived side by side. In future, too, we will have no alternative but to live as neighbours. I have, therefore, always attached great importance to our relationship. In this spirit I have sought to reach out to our Chinese brothers and sisters in the West as well as in Asia.

Scott Willis. Reprinted by permission of Copley News Service.

Furthermore, in my efforts to seek a negotiated solution to our problem, I have refrained from asking for the complete independence of Tibet. Historically and according to international law Tibet is an independent country under Chinese occupation. However, over the past sixteen years, since we established direct contact with the Beijing authorities in 1979, I have adopted a "middle-way" approach of reconciliation and compromise in the pursuit of a peaceful and negotiated resolution of the Tibetan issue. While it is the overwhelming desire of the Tibetan people to regain their national independence, I have repeatedly and publicly stated that I am willing to enter into negotiations on the basis of an agenda that does not include that independence. The continued occupation of Tibet poses an increasing threat to the very existence of a distinct Tibetan national and cultural identity. Therefore, I consider that my primary responsibility is to take whatever steps I must to save my people and their unique cultural heritage from total annihilation.

FORWARD TO THE FUTURE

Moreover, I believe that it is more important to look forward to the future than to dwell in the past. Theoretically speaking it is not impossible that the six million Tibetans could benefit from joining the one billion Chinese of their own free will, if a relationship based on equality, mutual benefit and mutual respect could be established. If China wants Tibet to stay with her, it is up to China to create the necessary conditions. But, the reality today is that Tibet is an occupied country under colonial rule. This is the essential issue which must be addressed and resolved through negotiations.

Unfortunately, the Chinese government has yet to accept any of the proposals and initiatives we have made over the years and has yet to enter into any substantive negotiations with us. Meanwhile, they continue to flood Tibet with Chinese immigrants, effectively reducing Tibetans to an insignificant minority in their own land. In fact some of my friends call this China's 'Final Solution' to the Tibetan problem.

THE NEED FOR URGENT ACTION

Tibet—an ancient nation with a unique culture and civilization—is disappearing fast. In endeavouring to protect my nation from this catastrophe, I have always sought to be guided by realism, moderation and patience. I have tried in every way I know to find some mutually acceptable solution in the spirit of reconciliation and compromise. However, it has now become clear that our efforts alone are not sufficient to bring the Chinese government to the negotiating table. I am, therefore, left with no other choice but to appeal to the international community for urgent intervention and action on behalf of my people.

In the first place, the true nature of China's rule over Tibet must be understood. China's leaders have for decades, even before the Communist revolution, propagated a false and self-serving version of the history of Tibet and of Tibet-China relations. Tibet's historical independence and its rich cultural and spiritual tradition have been entirely distorted to justify China's invasion, occupation and suppression of Tibet. The international community, and even the Chinese people, still does not fully comprehend the extent of the destruction, suffering and injustice experienced by the Tibetans under Chinese rule. Today the Chinese people, especially the intellectuals, closely follow what happens outside China.

The Chinese authorities are no longer able to isolate the population from outside sources of information. It is, therefore, immensely important that governments and non-governmental organisations in democratic countries discuss all aspects of the Tibetan issue, from the historical relations between Tibet and China to the current violations of human rights, openly and honestly.

Secondly, China's leaders must be made to realise that the question of Tibet will cause ever increasing problems to China domestically and internationally unless it is resolved to the satisfaction of both China and Tibet through earnest negotiations, in which all issues can be discussed with honesty and candour.

Thirdly, we need governments of democratic countries to continue to urge the Chinese authorities to respect human rights in Tibet and to enter into serious negotiations with us. We appeal for persistent and concerted efforts by the international community in bringing about direct and meaningful negotiations.

Fourthly, in their contacts with leaders and members of the democratic movement in China and in exile, governments of democratic countries should make clear their expectations with regard to China's future conduct towards Tibet. Now is the time for Chinese democrats to make commitments in this respect.

A NON-VIOLENT STRUGGLE

On our part, we Tibetans will continue our non-violent struggle for freedom. My people are calling for an intensification of the struggle, and I believe they will put this into effect. But we will resist the use of violence as an expression of the desperation which many Tibetans feel. As long as I lead our freedom struggle, there will be no deviation from the path of non-violence.

I remain committed to negotiations with China. In order to find a mutually acceptable solution, I have adopted a "middle-way" approach. This is also in response to, and within the framework of, Mr. Deng Xiaoping's stated assurance that "anything except independence can be discussed and resolved." I have formulated the basic ideas of "middle-way" approach in my former proposals, the Five Point Peace Plan (1987) and the Strasbourg Proposal in 1988. I regret very much that Mr. Deng Xiaoping [was not] able to translate his assurance into reality. However, I am hopeful that his successors will see the wisdom of resolving our problem peacefully through negotiations. These proposals were very well received internationally, and they can still form a rational basis for negotiations.

My framework for negotiations does not call for the independence of Tibet. What I am striving for is genuine self-rule for Tibet. Today I wish to reiterate our willingness to start negotiations with China anytime, anywhere without any preconditions. And I extend to China's leaders an invitation to open negotiations as soon as possible in the interests of both Tibetan and Chinese peoples.

| "Old Tibet under feudal serfdom was
one of the regions in the world with
the worst human rights records."

CHINESE RULE OVER TIBET SHOULD BE ACCEPTED

China Internet Information Center

China's governance of Tibet is beneficial and should be accepted by the international community, contends the China Internet Information Center in the following viewpoint. Contrary to the claims of Tibetan spiritual leaders, the authors argue, Tibet was a cruel religious dictatorship before the advent of democratic reforms enforced by China after 1959. Furthermore, the Information Center maintains, the current Dalai Lama (leader of the Tibetan Buddhists) has created a distorted version of Tibetan history and has used his title as a political tool to promote dangerous separatist activities against the Chinese government. The China Internet Information Center is a website run by the China International Book Trading Corporation.

As you read, consider the following questions:

1. Which historical facts reveal the validity of China's rule over Tibet, according to the authors?
2. How were Tibetan serfs and slaves treated prior to the 1959 democratic reforms in Tibet, according to the China Internet Information Center?
3. In the authors' opinion, how has the fourteenth Dalai Lama actually closed the door to negotiations with China?

Reprinted from the China Internet Information Center, "On the So-Called 'Tibetan Issue,'" at http://www.chinanews.org/cicc/jzm/single/english/e4.html, November 11, 1997, by permission.

Is Tibet an independent state? As early as in the 7th century, when China was under the rule of the Tang Dynasty (618–907), the Tibetan and the Han cemented close ties in the political, economic and cultural fields through imperial marriage and meetings. This paved the way for the later founding of a unified country. In the mid–13th century, Tibet was officially incorporated into China then under the rule of the Yuan Dynasty (1271–1368), becoming an administrative region directly under the Central Government. The Yuan emperor established the Xuanzheng (Political) Council in the Central Government to handle national Buddhist and Tibetan affairs, appointed Tibetan government and religious leaders as well as local officials, took census, and decided on taxation. In the ensuing centuries, China experienced changes in central political power. Tibet, however, remained under the rule of the Central Government.

GOVERNING TIBET

In the mid– and late–17th century, the Qing Dynasty (1644–1911) further tightened administration over Tibet by introducing the system for Tibetan Galoon officials to handle government affairs and stationing High Commissioners in Tibet. The 29-article Ordinance for the More Efficient Governing of Tibet, promulgated in 1792, contains explicit stipulations concerning the reincarnation of the Living Buddhas as well as the administrative, financial, military and foreign affairs of Tibet. The result is that the Central Government rule over Tibet became systemized and legalized. The Central Government issued certificates of appointment and seals of authority to the Dalai Lama and the Panchen Erdeni, making it possible for them to establish their leading position in Tibetan Buddhism.

Given cheating that existed in the incarnation of the Living Buddhas, which fueled strife, the Qing imperial court introduced the system of drawing lots from the golden urn to determine their reincarnated soul boys, and stipulated that the incarnation of the Living Buddhas, especially the Dalai Lama and the Panchen Erdeni, had to follow the lot-drawing system with the approval of the Central Government. The Central Government sent its representatives to chair and earmark money to cover their enthronement ceremony and the ceremony held for them to come to power in Tibet. This has evolved into a religious ritual and set historical system. Going against them is illegal. The Qing Central Government stationed High Commissioners in Tibet. On behalf of the Central Government, they were charged with supervising and handling Tibetan affairs, such as examining the annual financial income and expenditure of the Dalai Lama and the Panchen Erdeni, patrolling the various parts of the region, inspecting troops stationed in Tibet and boundary markers. They were fully empowered to deal with Tibet's foreign affairs. The Central Government appointed high-ranking Tibetan officials and paid them annual salaries, and sent people to manage Tibetan and Han troops. These facts show that the Central Government exercised effective governing of the administrative region of Tibet.

As the 14th Dalai Lama is impotent to negate the fact that Tibet remained under the Central Government prior to 1911, he turns to claim that after 1911 Tibet was "independent." However, how did he, then named Lhamo Toinzhol, become the 14th Dalai Lama Tenzin Gyatso? Historical archives say that he was located and determined as the reincarnated soul boy of the late 13th Dalai Lama in accordance with religious rituals and historical precedence. With approval from the Central Government, he was enthroned as the 14th Dalai Lama. The Central Government earmarked 400,000 silver dollars to cover the enthronement ceremony which was presided over by Chairman Wu Zhongxin of the Commission for Mongolian and Tibetan Affairs, who was sent there by the Nationalist Government. In the face of these historical facts, the 14th Dalai Lama is really not qualified to say Tibet was independent after 1911.

TIBET AND THE DALAI LAMA

What was Tibet like when it was under the rule by the 14th Dalai Lama? Prior to the Democratic Reform in 1959, Tibet, then under the rule by the 14th Dalai Lama, followed the system known as the temporal and religious administration. It was a feudal serfdom society, where monks and aristocrats exercised dictatorship over the broad masses of serfs and slaves more cruelly than in Europe during the Middle Ages.

At that time, the three estate-holders—officials, aristocrats and upper-class monks, who made up less than 5 percent of the Tibetan population—owned all the arable land, pastures, forests and mountains, and the bulk of livestock. Serfs and slaves were owned by serf owners just like the means of production. They were freely given away as gifts or for mortgage, sold or exchanged. The serf owners had the power to execute their serfs and slaves. Under the situation, the serfs and slaves had no personal freedom, suffering from cruel oppression and exploitation, and enjoying no human rights at all.

In old Tibet, the law stipulated in explicit terms and strictly defended the rigidly stratified unequal social system. The 13–Article Law and the 16–Article Law stipulated: "Man is classified into varied classes, so the value of their lives varies, too." While the life of a person of upper class was valued in gold amounting to the weight of his body, the life of a person of lower class, such as a woman, a butcher, a hunter or an artisan, was valued at a straw rope. Serf owners punished their serfs, when they violated the law, in an extremely savage and cruel way. The serf owners would strip those allegedly in light cases of their clothes and whip them in the public; for those allegedly in serious cases, the serf owners would gouge out their eyes, cut off their tongues, ears, hands or feet, pull out their tendon, skin them or throw them into scorpion caves.

The above facts show that old Tibet under feudal serfdom was one of the regions in the world with the worst human rights records. However, the 14th Dalai clique and the international anti-China forces refuse to recognize the fact. They describe the feudal serfdom enforced in old Tibet as the "holiest and the most beautiful system" in the world. Although the former Tibetan serfs and slaves enjoyed no human rights at all in old Tibet and have become masters of their own fate today, they say they have been deprived of human rights.

BUDDHISM AS POLITICAL TOOL

What kind of person is the 14th Dalai Llama? Can he represent the Tibetan people? The 14th Dalai Lama says he is a "kind" peace envoy, who refrains from killing even a fly. When he was performing Buddhist rituals, however, he demanded sacrificial objects including human skulls, human skins and fresh human intestines. In old Tibet under his rule, lots of serfs and slaves were either crippled or cruelly killed by serf owners. Armed rebellion and riots the 14th Dalai clique staged in Tibet took a heavy toll of innocent Tibetans.

The 14th Dalai, who styles himself "religious leader" of Tibetan Buddhism, does things against the set historical system and religious ritual. He left no stone unturned to meddle with and undermine efforts made, in accordance with religious rituals and historical precedence, to locate and determine the reincarnated soul boy of the late 10th Panchen Erdeni. When he staged "time of wheel abhiseka consecration ceremonies," he turned them into political rallies. Through "lecturing on Buddhist scriptures" and smuggling propaganda materials into Tibet, he tried to make a mess of monasteries. He incited monks and nuns, who were ignorant of truth, to engage in "Tibetan independence" activities. He even met five times Shoko Asahara, chief of the Aum Shinrikyo Sect of Japan which was notorious for its poison gas attack in Tokyo's subways on March 20, 1995. He said Shoko Asahara is a "friend" of his, and entrusted him to "propagate Buddhism" twice in Tibet. Facts testify to the truth that the 14th Dalai Lama is not promoting Tibetan Buddhism. Instead, he is using Tibetan Buddhism as a political tool for his separatist activities.

A Mockery of Democracy and Freedom

The Dalai Lama claims that he is only asking for Tibetan "autonomy," in an attempt to mislead the public.

The system of regional autonomy for ethnic minorities has in fact been in place in the Tibet Autonomous Region for more than 30 years. Under this system, the Tibetan people enjoy various rights, which they never enjoyed in old Tibet under the Dalai Lama's rule. . . .

It is odd that the Dalai Lama flaunts himself in pursuit of "democracy" and "freedom" and claims that "democracy" and "freedom" should be restored in Tibet. How could there have been democracy and freedom in old Tibet, where the Dalai Lama, the chief representative of the three categories of manorial lords, the former Tibet local government and the monasteries and nobility, exercised savage and dark rule?

The fact is that the Dalai Lama, who sets himself up as a defender of "democracy" and "freedom," constitutes a gross mockery of democracy and freedom.

China Internet Information Center, 1997.

Cloaked as "religious leader," the 14th Dalai Lama has been reduced to a politician-in-exile who attempts to mislead Tibetan Buddhism. Although he poses as a peace envoy who stands for "love and non-violence," he is actually the culprit of activities geared to undermine stability and unity and incite separatist riots in Tibet.

A Feudal Serfdom in Tibet?

The 14th Dalai Lama claims he is the representative of the Tibetan people. Actually, he is not the spokesman of the Tibetan people, simply because he is the representative of the feudal serfdom enforced in old Tibet. When he was ruling Tibet, the broad masses of the Tibetans yearned for an end to the cruel serfdom. And the savage feudal system characteristic of temporal and religious administration was truly abolished during the Democratic Reform in Tibet in 1959. The historical change ushered in a new page of life for the Tibetans. Those who groaned under the feudal serfdom have become masters of their own fate today. How could ex-serfs and ex-slaves, who are working for new Tibet, take the 14th Dalai Lama, the most important serf owner, as their spokesman? And how could such a serf owner represent his ex-serfs and ex-slaves, and speak for them?

As a matter of fact, the 14th Dalai Lama is representative of a small handful of his followers. These people were serf owners or upper-class aristocrats in old Tibet, who dream of reintroducing the feudal serfdom to Tibet so that they could re-ride roughshod over the broad masses of the Tibetans. As a result, the 14th Dalai Lama styles himself as the "spokesman of the Tibetan people" merely to mislead the public and win sympathy and support. In a nutshell, he is finding excuses for his "Tibetan independence" activities. . . .

CLOSING THE DOOR TO NEGOTIATIONS

The 14th Dalai Lama has demanded, off and on, "negotiation" with the Central Government. In the last few years, he did so wherever he went, in an attempt to convince all that the Central Government should be blamed for having held no negotiation with him over the past 10 years or more.

What kind of negotiation is the 14th Dalai Lama demanding? The Central Government managed to get in touch with the 14th Dalai Lama in 1978, but he failed to make arrangements for negotiation through this channel. He did demand negotiation with the Central Government, but he did so for the sake of propaganda. The 14th Dalai Lama raised his so-called "five-point plan" during his speech at the United States Congressional Human Rights Caucus in September 1987 and the "seven-point suggestion" during the press conference held in a meeting hall of the European Parliament Building in Strasbourg, France, in June 1988, declaring that these would be used as the basis for negotiation with the Central Government. However, both the "five-point plan" and the "seven-point suggestion" advocate "Tibetan independence" and stated that "Tibet was an independent state in history." Both mean to negate the fact that Tibet has since the Yuan Dynasty been a part of China and the Chinese Government boasts sovereignty over Tibet.

Riots that broke out in Lhasa in 1988 and 1989 were engineered, organized and supported by the people sent by the "government-in-exile" of the 14th Dalai clique. In 1989 when the 10th Panchen Erdeni demised, the Chinese department concerned invited the 14th Dalai Lama to return to attend the mourning activities. If the 14th Dalai Lama did have sincerity to enter into negotiation with the Central Government, he should have accepted the invitation totally out of religious purpose. Unfortunately, the 14th Dalai Lama refused to accept it. Instead, he did his best to undermine the reincarnation of the late 10th Panchen Erdeni, a holy event in Tibetan Buddhism. In total disregard of the religious rituals and historical precedence, he cheated to announce a Tibetan boy was the "soul boy" of the late master. In late 1993, the 14th Dalai Lama unilaterally announced an end to his contact with the Central Government. It is the 14th Dalai Lama who closed the door to contacts and negotiations.

Recent years saw the 14th Dalai Lama change his tactics by declaring that he only seeks "autonomy," instead of independence, in Tibet. By "autonomy," however, he means a rule exclusively by him and other serf owners who follow him to lead an exile life abroad, and "the autonomy which will lead to independence." The 14th Dalai Lama is still distorting Tibetan history in public, creating public opinion for his "Tibetan independence" move. In the summer of 1997, the 14th Dalai Lama distributed a pamphlet titled "Tibet: the Largest Colony in the World," which was produced by some Westerners. While demanding "negotiations" with the Central Government, the 14th Dalai Lama moved to collaborate with those who stand for the independence of Taiwan. Given this, one can hardly believe he has all the sincerity to negotiate with the Central Government.

PERIODICAL BIBLIOGRAPHY

The following articles have been selected to supplement the diverse views presented in this chapter. Addresses are provided for periodicals not indexed in the *Readers' Guide to Periodical Literature*, the *Alternative Press Index*, the *Social Sciences Index*, or the *Index to Legal Periodicals and Books*.

Barbara Crossette	"On Eve of U.N. Rwanda Trials, Reports of Misconduct," *New York Times*, January 9, 1997.
Economist	"Justice in Bosnia," February 17, 1996. Available from 111 W. 57th St., New York, NY 10019-2211.
Misha Glenny	"Will the West Fail Again?" *New York Times*, January 31, 1997.
Daniel Jonah Goldhagen	"The People's Holocaust," *New York Times*, March 17, 1996.
Jan Goodwin	"Rwanda: Justice Denied," *On the Issues*, Fall 1997.
Agnes Heller	"Natural Law and the Paradox of Evil," *Dissent*, Winter 1994.
Kenneth Jost	"War Crimes: Should an International Court Prosecute Atrocities?" *Congressional Quarterly*, July 7, 1995. Available from 1414 22nd St. NW, Washington, DC 20037.
Anthony Lewis	"Light in the Darkness," *New York Times*, December 9, 1996.
Saul Mendlovitz and John Fousek	"Enforcing the Law on Genocide," *Alternatives*, April–June 1996.
Jo-Ann Mort	"Anne Frank and Bosnia," *Dissent*, Winter 1997.
Paul Murphy	"Tale of Two Tibets," *World & I*, June 1997. Available from 3600 New York Ave. NE, Washington, DC 20002.
Stephen R. Shalom	"The Rwanda Genocide: The Nightmare That Happened," *Z Magazine*, April 1996.
Sara Wood	"Should We Have a Permanent International Criminal Court?" *Human Rights*, Winter 1996. Available from the ABA Press for the Section of Individual Rights and Responsibilities of the American Bar Association, 750 N. Lake Shore Dr., Chicago, IL 60611.

FOR FURTHER DISCUSSION

CHAPTER 1

1. Pierre Sané contends that all nations should adhere to internationally defined standards on human rights. Bilahari Kausikan argues that such standards often ignore Asian nations' cultural values. Sané is the secretary general of Amnesty International and Kausikan is a diplomat from Singapore. How are the backgrounds of these two authors evident in their views about the validity of universal human rights? How does knowing their backgrounds influence your assessment of their arguments? Explain your answer.

2. Robert Weil asserts that the Chinese highly value certain economic rights—particularly government-guaranteed jobs, health care, and housing—that receive less emphasis in Western nations. What argument does Xiaorong Li offer in response to the claim that Asian cultures often value economic rights over political rights? Which author's argument is more convincing? Why?

3. Hillary Rodham Clinton contends that the struggle for women's rights must become a part of the international human rights agenda. Anne Applebaum maintains that Western supporters of women's rights have often downplayed the human rights concerns of third world women. Compare the opinions presented in these two viewpoints, then formulate your own assessment of the contemporary state of human rights for women.

CHAPTER 2

1. How does Midge Decter respond to John Shattuck's claim that the United States faces serious human rights challenges? Does her viewpoint effectively refute Shattuck's contention? Why or why not?

2. Bruce Weiner uses historical information and data from labor organizations, activists, and experts to support his argument that the use of child labor violates human rights. Shahidul Alam incorporates the opinions of child workers to back up his contention that humanitarian efforts to end the use of child labor are counterproductive. Which author's technique do you find more compelling? Why?

3. Amnesty International argues that refugees face increasing barriers to political asylum, while David Simcox contends that too many people are given asylum on the basis of unwarranted claims of persecution. What evidence does each author present

to support his or her argument? Which author's use of evidence do you find more convincing? Explain.

4. Karen J. Longstreth and Bernard E. Trainor disagree about the need for a global ban on the use of antipersonnel land mines. Do you believe that there should be an international ban on the use of land mines? Why or why not? Support your answer with evidence from the viewpoints.

CHAPTER 3

1. Robert F. Drinan contends that nongovernmental organizations (NGOs) are effective crusaders for human rights, while Alexander Cockburn maintains that most NGOs are ineffective. How do the arguments of these two authors reflect differing views on the goals of human rights activism?

2. Abigail McCarthy argues that the list of minimum standards drafted by a U.S. governmental commission will help prevent human rights abuses in overseas factories. Medea Benjamin contends that these standards will not protect factory workers' human rights. In your opinion, which of these authors presents a stronger case? Explain your answer, using examples from the viewpoints.

3. Katha Pollitt and Wayne Lutton disagree about the need to extend political asylum to female refugees. Each author uses the case of Fauziya Kasinga, a woman who asked for asylum to escape the practice of female genital mutilation, as a supporting example. Compare the use of Kasinga's case in Pollitt's viewpoint with that in Lutton's viewpoint. In your opinion, which author uses the example of Kasinga's case to better effect?

4. James A. Dorn argues that free trade advances human rights in China; Harry Wu disagrees. Dorn is affiliated with the Cato Institute, a research foundation that promotes capitalist economics; Wu spent nearly twenty years as a political prisoner in China's labor camps. Does knowing their backgrounds influence your evaluation of their arguments? Explain.

CHAPTER 4

1. The viewpoints in this chapter include several recommendations on actions that should be taken in response to genocide and crimes against humanity. Consider each recommendation and then list arguments for and against each one. Note whether the arguments are based on facts, values, emotions, or other considerations. If you believe a recommendation should not be considered at all, reveal why.

2. Tenzin Gyatso argues that the international community should

intervene in the Tibetan-Chinese conflict to prevent the "cultural genocide" of the Tibetan people. The China Internet Information Center contends that China's governance of Tibet benefits the Tibetan people and should therefore be supported by the international community. In your opinion, which author presents the most convincing argument? Support your answer with examples from the viewpoints.

ORGANIZATIONS TO CONTACT

The editors have compiled the following list of organizations concerned with the issues debated in this book. The descriptions are derived from materials provided by the organizations. All have publications or information available for interested readers. The list was compiled on the date of publication of the present volume; the information provided here may change. Be aware that many organizations take several weeks or longer to respond to inquiries, so allow as much time as possible.

American Civil Liberties Union (ACLU)
125 Broad St., 18th Fl., New York, NY 10004
(212) 549-2500 • fax: (212) 549-2646
web address: http://www.aclu.org
The ACLU is a national organization that works to defend Americans' civil rights guaranteed by the U.S. Constitution. The ACLU publishes and distributes policy statements, pamphlets, and the semiannual newsletter *Civil Liberties Alert*.

American Immigration Control Foundation (AICF)
PO Box 525, Monterey, VA 24465
(540) 468-2022 • fax: (540) 468-2024
e-mail: aicf@cfw.com • web address:
http://www.cfw.com/~aicf
The AICF is a research and educational organization whose primary goal is to promote a reasonable immigration policy based on national interests and needs. The foundation educates the public on what its members believe are the disastrous effects of uncontrolled immigration. It publishes the monthly newsletter *Border Watch* as well as several monographs and books on the historical, legal, and demographic aspects of immigration.

Amnesty International (AI)
322 8th Ave., New York, NY 10001
(212) 807-8400 • fax: (212) 627-1451
web address: http://www.amnesty—usa.org
Amnesty International is a worldwide, independent voluntary movement that works to free people detained for their beliefs who have not used or advocated violence and people imprisoned because of their ethnic origin, sex, language, national or social origin, economic status, and birth or other status. AI seeks

to ensure fair and prompt trials for political prisoners and to abolish torture, "disappearances," cruel treatment of prisoners, and executions. Its publications include a quarterly newsletter, *Amnesty Action*, an annual book, *Amnesty International Report*, and various briefing papers and special reports.

Cato Institute
1000 Massachusetts Ave. NW, Washington, DC 20001-5403
(202) 842-0200, fax: (202) 842-3490
web address: http://www.cato.org

The Cato Institute is a libertarian public policy research foundation dedicated to limiting the role of government and protecting individual liberties. The institute publishes the quarterly magazine *Regulation*, the bimonthly *Cato Policy Report*, and numerous books.

Child Labor Coalition (CLC)
c/o National Consumers League
1701 K St., NW, Suite 1200, Washington, DC 20006
(202) 835-3323, fax: (202) 835-0747
e-mail: NCLNCL@aol.com, web address: http://www.essential.org

The CLC serves as a national network for the exchange of information about child labor. It provides a forum for groups seeking to protect working minors and to end the exploitation of child labor. It works to influence public policy on child labor issues, to protect youths from hazardous work, and to advocate for better enforcement of child labor laws. The CLC publishes the newsletter *Child Labor Monitor* several times a year.

Global Exchange
2017 Mission St., No. 303, San Francisco, CA 94110
(415) 255-7296, (800) 497-1994, fax: (415) 255-7498
e-mail: gx-info@globalexchange.org
web address: http://www.globalexchange.org

Global Exchange is a nonprofit organization that promotes social justice, environmental sustainability, and grassroots activism on international human rights issues. Global Exchange produces various books, videos, and other educational programs and materials concerning human rights.

Heritage Foundation
214 Massachusetts Ave. NE, Washington, DC 20002
(202) 546-4400, fax: (202) 546-8328

web address: http://www.heritage.org

The Heritage Foundation is a conservative public policy research institute that advocates free-market economics and limited government. Its publications include the monthly *Policy Review*, the *Backgrounder* series of occasional papers, and the *Heritage Lectures* series.

Human Rights and Race Relations Centre
Suite 500, 120 Eglinton Ave. East, Toronto, ON M4P 1E2, CANADA
phone and fax: (416) 481-7793

The centre is a registered charity organization that opposes all types of discrimination. It strives to develop a society free of racism where each ethnic group respects the rights of other groups. It recognizes individuals and institutions that excel in the promotion of race relations or that work for the elimination of discrimination. The centre publishes the weekly newspaper *New Canada*.

Human Rights Watch
485 Fifth Ave., New York, NY 10017-6104
(212) 972-8400, fax: (212) 972-0905
e-mail: hrwnyc@hrw.org, web address: http://www.hrw.org

Human Rights Watch regularly investigates human rights abuses in over seventy countries around the world. It promotes civil liberties and defends freedom of thought, due process, and the equal protection of the law. Its goal is to hold governments accountable for human rights violations they commit against individuals because of their political, ethnic, or religious affiliations. It publishes the *Human Rights Watch Quarterly Newsletter*, the annual *Human Rights Watch World Report*, and a semiannual publications catalog.

International Campaign for Tibet (ICT)
1825 K St. NW, Suite 520, Washington, DC 20006
(202) 785-1515, fax: (202) 785-4343
e-mail: ict@peacenet.org, web address:
http://www.savetibet.org

ICT is a nonpartisan, nonprofit organization dedicated to promoting human rights and democratic freedoms for the people of Tibet. It sponsors fact-finding missions to Tibet, works in conjunction with the UN and the U.S. Congress to protect Tibetan culture, and promotes educational and media coverage of human rights issues in Tibet. ICT publishes two newsletters, the *Tibet Press Watch*, published six times a year, and the *Tibetan Environment & Development News*, published at various times throughout the year.

International Labour Office (ILO)
Washington Branch
1828 L Street NW, Washington, DC 20036
(202) 653-7652, fax: (202) 653-7687
e-mail: ilowbo@aol.com, web address: http://www.ilo.org

The ILO works to promote basic human rights through improved working and living conditions by enhancing opportunities for those who are excluded from meaningful salaried employment. The ILO pioneered such landmarks of industrial society as the eight-hour work day, maternity protection, and workplace safety regulations. It runs the ILO Publications Bureau, which publishes various policy statements and background information on all aspects of employment. *World Employment* and *Child Labour: Targeting the Intolerable* are examples of ILO publications.

National Consumers League (NCL)
1701 K St. NW, Suite 1200, Washington, DC 20006
(202) 835-3323, fax: (202) 835-0747
e-mail: NCLNCL@aol.com
web address: http://www.natlconsumersleague.org

Founded in 1899, NCL is the nation's pioneer consumer group which works to bring consumer power to bear on marketplace and workplace issues. NCL worked for the first minimum wage laws, overtime compensation, and the child labor provisions in the Fair Labor Standards Act. It also helped organize the Child Labor Coalition, which is committed to ending child labor exploitation in the U.S. and abroad. NCL publishes various articles on U.S. and international child labor and the newsletter *NCL Bulletin*, published six times a year.

National Network for Immigrant and Refugee Rights (NNIRR)
310 Eighth St., Suite 307, Oakland, CA 94607-4253
(510) 465-1984, fax: (510) 465-1885
e-mail: nnirr@nnirr.org, web address: http://www.nnirr.org

The network includes community, church, labor, and legal groups committed to the cause of equal rights for all immigrants. These groups work to end discrimination against and unfair treatment of illegal immigrants and refugees. The network aims to strengthen and coordinate educational efforts among immigration advocates nationwide. It publishes a quarterly newsletter, Network News.

United Nations Association of the USA (UNA-USA)

801 Second Ave., 2nd Fl., New York, NY 10017-4706
(212) 907-1300, fax: (212) 682-9185
e-mail: unany@igc.apc.org, web address:
http://www.unausa.org

UNA-USA is the largest grassroots foreign policy organization in the United States and the nation's leading center of policy research on the UN and global issues. It works with the UN to identify better ways in which the international community can use its resources to respond to pressing human needs, such as international terrorism, emergency relief, and human rights. It publishes the quarterly newspaper The Inter Dependent, the annual book A Global Agenda: Issues Before the General Assembly of the United Nations, and the Washington Weekly Report.

BIBLIOGRAPHY OF BOOKS

Mahnaz Afkhami, ed.   *Faith and Freedom: Women's Human Rights in the Muslim World.* Syracuse, NY: Syracuse University Press, 1995.

Philip Alston, ed.   *Promoting Human Rights Through Bills of Rights: Comparative Perspectives.* New York: Clarendon Press, 1997.

Amnesty International   *Human Rights Are Women's Right.* New York: Amnesty International USA, 1995.

Amnesty International   *Rwanda and Burundi, the Return Home: Rumours and Realities.* New York: Amnesty International USA, 1996.

George J. Andreopoulos, ed.   *Genocide: Conceptual and Historical Dimensions.* Philadelphia: University of Pennsylvania Press, 1997.

Irene Bloom,
J. Paul Martin, and
Wayne L. Proudfoot, eds.   *Religious Diversity and Human Rights.* New York: Columbia University Press, 1996.

Norberto Bobbio   *The Age of Rights.* Cambridge, MA: Polity Press, 1996.

Youcef Bouandel   *Human Rights and Comparative Politics.* Brookfield, VT: Dartmouth, 1997.

Marguerite Guzman Bouvard   *Women Reshaping Human Rights: How Extraordinary Activists Are Changing the World.* Wilmington, DE: Scholarly Resources, 1996.

Alan E. Boyle and
Michael R. Anderson, eds.   *Human Rights Approaches to Environmental Protection.* New York: Clarendon Press, 1996.

Edward L. Cleary   *The Struggle for Human Rights in Latin America.* Westport, CT: Praeger, 1997.

Rebecca J. Cook, ed.   *Human Rights of Women: National and International Perspectives.* Philadelphia: University of Pennsylvania Press, 1994.

Mary Craig   *Tears of Blood: A Cry for Tibet.* London: HarperCollins, 1992.

Francis M. Deng   *Protecting the Dispossessed: A Challenge for the International Community.* Washington, DC: Brookings, 1993.

Alain Destexhe   *Rwanda and Genocide in the Twentieth Century.* New York: New York University Press, 1995.

Siobahn Dowd, ed.   *This Prison Where I Live: The Pen Anthology of Imprisoned Writers.* New York: Cassell Academic, 1996.

Glynne Evans   *Responding to Crises in the African Great Lakes.* New York: Oxford University Press for the International Institute for Strategic Studies, 1997.

William Felice	*Taking Suffering Seriously:The Importance of Collective Human Rights.* Albany: State University of New York Press, 1996.
Duncan Forrest	*A Glimpse of Hell: Reports on TortureWorldwide.* New York: New York University Press, 1996.
Johan Galtung	*Human Rights in Another Key.* Cambridge, MA: Polity Press, 1994.
Daniel Jonah Goldhagen	*Hitler'sWilling Executioners: Ordinary Germans and the Holocaust.* New York: Knopf, 1996.
Hurst Hannum and Dana D. Fisher, eds.	*U.S. Ratification of the International Covenants on Human Rights.* Irvington-on-Hudson, NY: Transnational, 1993.
Rhoda E. Howard	*Human Rights and the Search for Community.* Boulder, CO: Westview Press, 1995.
Olwen Hufton, ed.	*Historical Change and Human Rights:The Oxford Amnesty Lectures 1994.* New York: BasicBooks, 1995.
Human Rights Watch	*The Human RightsWatch Global Report on Prisons.* New York: Human Rights Watch, 1993.
Human Rights Watch/ Helsinki	*Bosnia and Hercegovina:The Unindicted, Reaping the Rewards of "Ethnic Cleansing."* New York: Human Rights Watch/Helsinki, 1997.
Human Rights Watch Women's Rights Project	*The Global Report on Women's Rights.* Washington, DC: Yale University Press, 1996.
Micheline R. Ishay, ed.	*The Human Rights Reader: Major Political Essays, Speeches, and Documents from the Bible to the Present.* New York: Routledge, 1997.
David Jacobson	*Rights Across Borders: Immigration and the Decline of Citizenship.* Baltimore: Johns Hopkins University Press, 1996.
Kurt Jonassohn and Karin Solveig Bjornson	*Genocide and Gross Human RightsViolations.* New Brunswick, NJ: Transaction, 1997.
Peter Juviler et al., eds.	*Human Rights for the 21st Century: Foundations for Responsible Hope.* Armonk, NY: M.E. Sharpe, 1993.
Neil Jeffrey Kressel	*Mass Hate:The Global Rise of Genocide and Terror.* New York: Plenum Press, 1996.
Susan Kuklin	*Irrepressible Spirit: Conversations with Human Rights Activists.* New York: Philomel Books, 1996.
Dalai Lama	*Freedom in Exile:The Autobiography of the Dalai Lama.* New York: HarperCollins, 1991.
Gil Loescher and Ann Dull Loescher	*The Global Refugee Crisis: A Reference Handbook.* Santa Barbara, CA: ABC-CLIO, 1994.

Kathleen E. Mahoney and Paul Mahoney, eds. *Human Rights in the Twenty-First Century: A Global Challenge*. Boston: M. Nijhoff, 1993.

Oliver Mendelsohn and Upendra Baxi, eds. *The Rights of Subordinated Peoples*. New York: Oxford University Press, 1994.

Christopher Merrill *The Old Bridge: The Third Balkan War and the Age of the Refugee*. Minneapolis: Milkweed Editions, 1995.

Julie Mertus, ed. *The Suitcase: Refugee Voices from Bosnia and Croatia*. Berkeley and Los Angeles: University of California Press, 1997.

R.A. Mullerson *Human Rights Diplomacy*. New York: Routledge, 1997.

Julie Stone Peters and Andrea Wolper, eds. *Women's Rights, Human Rights: International Feminist Perspectives*. New York: Routledge, 1995.

Anthony H. Richmond *Global Apartheid: Refugees, Racism, and the New World Order*. Toronto: Oxford University Press, 1994.

Shawn Roberts and Jody Williams *After the Guns Fall Silent: The Enduring Legacy of Landmines*. Washington, DC: Vietnam Veterans of America Foundation, 1995.

Naomi Roht-Arriaza, ed. *Impunity and Human Rights in International Law and Practice*. New York: Oxford University Press, 1995.

Robert I. Rotberg and Thomas G. Weiss, eds. *From Massacres to Genocide: The Media, Public Policy, and Humanitarian Crises*. Washington, DC: Brookings, 1996.

Jamil Salmi *Violence and Democratic Society: New Approaches to Human Rights*. London: Zed Books, 1993.

Austin Sarat and Thomas R. Kearns, eds. *Identities, Politics, and Rights*. Ann Arbor: University of Michigan Press, 1995.

Stephen Shute and Susan Hurley, eds. *On Human Rights*. New York: BasicBooks, 1993.

Tara Smith *Moral Rights and Political Freedom*. Lanham, MD: Rowman & Littlefield, 1995.

Henry J. Steiner and Philip Alston *International Human Rights in Context: Law, Politics, Morals*. New York: Oxford University Press, 1996.

Howard B. Tolley Jr. *The International Commission of Jurists: Global Advocates for Human Rights*. Philadelphia: University of Pennsylvania Press, 1994.

Samuel Totten, William S. Parsons, and Israel W. Charny, eds. *Century of Genocide: Eyewitness Accounts and Critical Views*. New York: Garland, 1997.

Alex Vines *Still Killing: Landmines in Southern Africa*. New York: Human Rights Watch, 1997.

Myron Weiner

The Global Migration Crisis: Challenge to States and to Human Rights. New York: HarperCollins College, 1995.

Lloyd L. Weinreb

Oedipus at Fenway Park: What Rights Are and Why There Are Any. Cambridge, MA: Harvard University Press, 1994.

Robert Wintemute

Sexual Orientation and Human Rights: The United States Constitution, the European Convention, and the Canadian Charter. New York: Oxford University Press, 1995.

Harry Wu with George Vecsey

Troublemaker: One Man's Crusade Against China's Cruelty. New York: Times Books, 1996.

Radmila Manojlovic Zarkovic and Fran Peavey, eds.

I Remember=Sjecam Se: Writings by Bosnian Women Refugees. San Francisco: Aunt Lute Books, 1996.

INDEX

abortion, 71
Abshire, David M., 153
Adams, Cathie, 55
Adorno, Theodore, 175
Afghanistan
    asylum seekers from, 93
    land mines in, 109
Africa
    female genital mutilation in, 138
    refugee crisis in, 89-90
Alam, Shahidul, 81
Algeria, 138
Amnesty International, 88
    founding of, 119, 137
    proposal on human rights protection,
        20
antipersonnel mines. *See* land mines
Applebaum, Anne, 51
Argentina, 119
asylum laws
    carrier sanctions under, 93-94
    protection under
        inadequacies of, 91-97
        scope of, 100-101
    shopping for nations with most
        desirable, 104-105
    steps to reform, 102-107
asylum seekers
    detention of, 95
        in U.S., 96
    many claims of are unwarranted, 98-
        107
    numbers admitted into U.S., 100-
        101, 142
    persecuted classes of, have expanded,
        100, 143
    political, barriers to, 88-97
    and refugees, distinction between,
        99, 142, 147
    treatment of, 18
        in Turkey, 92-93
    see also refugees
atrocity myths, 184
Avebury, Sir Eric, 119
Aylwin, Patricio, 186

Balladur, Edouard, 22
Bangladesh Rural Advancement
    Committee, 85
Beasley, Michele, 143
Benenson, Peter, 119
Benjamin, Medea, 131

Bosnia, 175
    atrocity myths in, 184
    coming to terms with past in, 186
    failure of international tribunal in,
        170, 171
    human rights abuses in, 23
    land mines in, 109
    refugee crisis in, 89-90
Brooks, Geraldine, 135
Browning, Christopher, 174
Buddhism
    as political tool in Tibet, 197-98
Buruma, Ian, 185
Bush, George, 136

Cambodia
    land mines in, 109
Carter, Jimmy, 106, 136, 165
Castro, Fidel, 158
Chesler, Ellen, 47
child labor
    extent of, 75, 76-77
    in Indonesia, 78-79
    in Pakistan, 79-80
    reasons for, 77-78, 86
    strategies for ending, 80
    violates human rights, 74-80
        con, 81-87
    what working children want, 84
Child Labor Deterrence Act
    is protective of U.S. trade interests, 82
Chile
    impact of Amnesty International in,
        119-20
China
    democracy movement in, 153
        consequences for Tibet, 189
    trade will not promote, 158-59
    economic sanctions against are
        ineffective, 152
    family limitation law in, 100, 136
    has distorted Tibetan history, 191-92
    rule over Tibet should be accepted,
        194-200
        con, 187-93
    should be admitted into World Trade
        Organization, 154
China Internet Information Center, 194
Chinese Communist Party
    nationalist trend in, 156-57
Chinese White Paper, 36
Christopher, Warren, 19, 26

Cithongo, Wanjiru, 54
Clinton, Hillary Rodham, 44
Clinton administration
  asylum policies of, 145
  on Chinese emigration, 106
  efforts to promote factory standards,
    129, 132
  policy on land mines, 111
  on trade sanctions on China, 32
clitoridectomy, 137
  see also female genital mutilation
Cockburn, Alexander, 123
cold war, 17
  U.S. political asylum policies during,
    136
Coleman, James, 72
Constitution, U.S.
  as blueprint for human rights, 63-64
Croatia
  land mines in, 109
cruelty, human
  investigation of, may prevent future
    atrocities, 173-80
  ordinary people are capable of, 174-
    75
Cuba, 136
Cuban Adjustment Act (1966), 106
cultural relativism, 41
cultural values
  vs. human rights, 17

Dalai Lama, 187, 195
  rule under, Chinese view of, 196-97
death penalty, 18, 70, 120
Decter, Midge, 67
Deng Xiaoping, 156, 192, 193
Disney
  wages paid by, 132
Dorn, James A., 149
Drinan, Robert F., 118
Dunlop, Joan, 47
Durkheim, Emile, 177

economic development
  as human right, 40-41
  vs. human rights, 17, 18
  rights of Third World countries to,
    31-32
Equality Now, 137
ethnic tensions, 19

factories
  minimum standards for
    should be adhered to, 127-30
    will not prevent abuses, 131-34

Faiz, Faiz Ahmad, 20
Fein, Bruce, 169
female circumcision, 53
female genital mutilation (F.G.M.),
    136, 137
  as cultural right, 146-47
  governments do not force on women,
    144
free trade
  is human right, 151
  promotes human rights in China,
    149-54
  con, 155-61
Friedan, Betty, 52
Friedrich Naumann Foundation, 188

garment factories
  child labor in, 85-86
genetic fallacy, 36-37
genocide
  cultural, in Tibet, 188-89
  investigation into human cruelty will
    help prevent, 173-80
Germany
  asylum system in, 102
Gifford, Kathie Lee, 75
Goldhagen, Daniel Jonah, 176
Greer, Germaine, 137
Grotius, Hugo, 61, 69
Gyatso, Tenzin, 187

Haitian refugees, 106
Hardin, Garrett, 147
Harkin, Tom, 81
Helsinki Accords, 124
Henkin, Louis, 65
Herbert, Bob, 129
Hinduism
  and asylum claims in India, 102
Hitchcock, David, 23
Hoess, Rudolf, 177
Holocaust
  and ordinary Germans, 176-79
homosexuals
  extenuation of asylum protection to,
    100
human rights
  abuses
    morality issues, 172
    ordinary people are capable of, 174-
      75
    in U.S., 64-65
  are universal, 17-20
  Chinese attitude toward, 27
  concept originated in West, 41

movement, 38
  Amnesty International's role in, 120
  universal definition of
    ignores cultural diversity, 21-24
    is relevant to Asian societies, 33-43
    neglects Asian values, 25-32

Ignatieff, Michael, 181, 184
immigration
  humanitarian, 99
  into U.S., 70
  asylum seekers only small part of,
    140
Immigration and Naturalization
  Service, 136
  bias of, against sex-based claims, 139
incarceration
  rates in U.S., 30
Indonesia
  child labor in, 78-79
International Covenant on Civil and
  Political Rights, 61, 62-63
  annual report required by, 68
International Covenant on Economic,
  Social, and Cultural Rights, 61
International Labor Organization, 61
  on child labor, 75-76
  Program on Elimination of Child
    Labor, 79
International War Crimes Tribunal
  on atrocities in Bosnia, 166
  failure of, 170, 171
  see also tribunals, international
Iraq
  land mines in, 109
Islam, 19, 52
  fundamentalism and asylum claims,
    102
  by women, 139

Jixuan Hu, 154
John Paul II, 111
Jordan, Michael, 75

Karadzic, Radovan, 170
Kasinga, Fauziya, 136, 138, 145-46
Katz, Fred E., 173
Kausikan, Bilahari, 21, 23
Khan, Kamran Aslam, 128

land mines
  cost of removing, 110
  countries producing, 110
  numbers of, 109
  use of

outlawing, would be futile, 112-14
  violates human rights, 108-11
language rights, 71
League of Nations, 61
Leahy, Patrick J., 113
Li, Xiaorong, 33
Lifton, Robert Jay, 176
Locke, John, 61, 69
Longstreth, Karen J., 108
Lutton, Wayne, 141

Mariel boat lift, 106, 136
Masih, Iqbal, 79, 128
McCarthy, Abigail, 127
Mengele, Josef, 177
Miller, George, 130
Mladic, Ratko, 170

Nada (Saudi asylum seeker), 140
nationalism, 19
Native Americans
  treatment of, by U.S., 70, 71
Nazi Doctors, The (Lifton), 176
Nazi war crimes
  and ordinary Germans, 176-79
  treatment of, vs. Soviet war crimes,
    170-71
Neier, Aryeh, 124
New York Times, 30, 32
NGOs. See nongovernmental
  organizations
Nike, 75, 76
  wages paid by, 132
Niskanen, William, 154
nongovernmental organizations, 45
  are ineffective, 123-26
  combat human rights abuses, 118-22
Nuremberg trials, 61, 170
  failure of, 185

Ordinary People and Extraordinary Evil (Katz),
  177

Pakistan
  asylum seekers in, 93
  child labor in, 79-80, 128
Panchen Erdeni, 195
Parkman, Francis, 71
persecuted classes
  under asylum protection, 100
Pinochet, Augusto, 119, 186
police brutality
  in U.S., 63
political asylum, 99
  should be granted to persecuted

women, 135-40
con, 141-48
political rights
vs. economic development, 17, 18
is false dilemma, 39-41
Pollitt, Katha, 135

refoulement, 91
Refugee Act (1980), 142
refugees
gaps in international protection for, 91-94
most are women and children, 89
numbers of
in Asia, Africa, and Europe, 92
protection of, is needed, 96-97
social benefits for
legislation limiting, 95
see also asylum seekers
Reich, Robert, 129
Reno, Janet, 143
rights
community vs. individual, 35-36
Robb, James S., 101
Romania, 136
asylum seekers from, 94
Rosen, Jeffrey, 146
Rwanda, 175
genocide in, 166
ineffectivity of NGOs in, 124-26
refugee crisis in, 90
special tribunal for war crimes in, 167
failure of, 170

Sané, Pierre, 17
Saudi Arabia, 140
Schwarzkopf, Norman, 111
Sen, Amartya, 40
Sex and Destiny (Greer), 137
Shattuck, John, 60, 68, 69
Simcox, David, 98
Somalia
land mines in, 109
South Africa
Truth and Reconciliation Commission in, 182, 184
Soviet war crimes
treatment of, vs. Nazi war crimes, 170-71
Stalin, Joseph, 170
Staub, Ervin, 176
Sykes, Charles J., 72

Tiananmen Square massacre, 26, 154,
157
Tibet, 53
cultural genocide in, 188-89
history of
China has distorted, 191-92
Chinese interpretation of, 195-96
international community should
intervene on behalf of, 187-93
con, 194-200
Trainor, Bernard E., 112
tribunals, international
attempt to individualize guilt, 185
benefits of, 167
failures of, 170
should be established, 165-68
con, 169-72
special, problems with, 166-67
will not alleviate suffering, 181-86
see also International War Crimes
Tribunal; Nuremberg trials
truth commissions, 182
require strong political consensus, 183
Turkey
treatment of asylum seekers in, 92-93
Tutu, Desmond, 111, 182
Tynan, Lynn M., 137

United Nations
ad hoc war crimes tribunals of, 170
birth of, 62
United Nations Conference on
Disarmament, 111
United Nations Fourth Conference on
Women, 52
United Nations Refugee Convention, 90
United Nations Universal Declaration
of Human Rights, 20, 23, 61, 62, 69
United Nations World Conference on
Human Rights, 120
United States
faces human rights challenges, 60-66
human rights violations in, 64-65
police brutality, 63
hypocrisy of
on child labor, 86-87
on human rights, 28-30
con, 67-73
immigration into, 70
is worldwide lure for asylum seekers, 99
policy on land mines, 111
political asylum policies during cold
war, 136

rhetoric of, spurs asylum seekers,
105-106
should follow policy of restraint with
China, 160-61
USA Today, 145
U.S. Campaign to Ban Landmines, 111

values
Asian
community vs. individuality, 38-39
debate over, 34
international human rights
standards neglect, 25-32
significance of, 22
cultural, 17
victimization
politics of, 72
victims
are least able to speak out, 39
Violence Against Women Act, 143

Waal, Alex de, 124
Wages of Guilt (Buruma), 185
Wal-Mart, 75, 76

Walsh, James H., 146
Washington Post, 146, 154
Weil, Robert, 25
Weiner, Bruce, 74
Welsh, Stephanie, 138
Wirths, Eduard, 176-77
women
choices of, must be respected, 48
extenuation of asylum protection to,
100
work of, is undervalued, 47
women's rights
agenda ignores Third World concerns,
51-56
human rights agenda must include,
44-50
movement in U.S., 50, 65
World Trade Organization
China should be admitted into, 154
Wu, Harry, 154, 155

Yalta accords, 170
Yugoslavia, 114
refugee crisis from breakup of, 90